# The Complete Book of Resistance Training

# The Complete Book of

# RESISTANCE TRAINING

## TONY LYCHOLAT

The Crowood Press

First published in 1990 by
The Crowood Press
Gipsy Lane, Swindon
Wiltshire SN21 6DQ

**British Library Cataloguing in Publication Data**

Lycholat, Tony
   The complete book of resistance training.
   I. Title
   613.71

ISBN 1 85223 394 X

Photo Credits
All warming-up and stretching exercises photographed by Jeremy
Enness and provided by Kaleidoscope Customer Services. In the
body-weight exercise section, illustrations courtesy of *Today's
Runner*/Angus Murray and Nike/David Hewitson. In the barbell/
dumb-bell exercise section, illustrations by Roy Wooding and
courtesy of *Today's Runner*/Angus Murray. Fig 1 Allsport/Bob
Martin. Figs 2 and 3 *Today's Runner*/Angus Murray. Fig 4 Keiser.
Fig 5 Allsport/Steve Powell. Fig 6 Powersport.

Typeset by Chippendale Type Limited, Otley, West Yorkshire.
Printed and bound in Great Britain by BPCC Hazell Books Ltd, Aylesbury.

# Contents

| | | |
|---|---|---:|
| | Acknowledgements | 6 |
| | Introduction | 7 |
| 1 | Understanding Muscle | 18 |
| 2 | Self-Assessment and Training Aims Analysis | 27 |
| 3 | Training Programmes | 31 |
| 4 | Warming Up and Warming Down for Resistance Training | 48 |
| 5 | Resistance-Training Exercises | 57 |
| | Appendices | 89 |
| | Further Reading | 95 |
| | Index | 96 |

# Acknowledgements

This book is the last in the series of four on the topic of fitness and training. Like the previous three titles and every other publication I have written, it has involved all kinds of people in all kinds of ways. With regard to the many illustrations, thanks must go to the photographers Jeremy Enness, Roy Wooding, David Hewitson and Angus Murray for taking such good photographs. Naturally, thanks must also go to the people who were kind enough to be photographed, namely Derek Redmond (courtesy of Nike) and Tim Hutchings (courtesy of Reebok). As far as the content of this book is concerned, this title would not exist without the patience and motivation of everybody who has at one time or another been a training partner, particularly Robert, Cherie and Michelle, as well as my most recent four-legged training friends, Pascal and Sparky! As ever, thanks must go to Flo who has kept the writing process going (for several years now) with the best tea in the world. Finally, my warmest thanks are reserved for Jenni, who continually kept my head from exploding, dragged me out of my frequent bouts of writer's depression, made me laugh about it and essentially did exactly the right things at exactly the right time – and that's not easy! Thanks.

# Introduction

Throughout the last ten years there has been a massive rise in the number of people who now perform some kind of resistance (or weight) training. Virtually all sports and leisure centres, health clubs and fitness facilities now feature some kind of resistance-training equipment, which is used by both the general public and sportsmen and women of all ages.

There are many reasons for the rapid rise in popularity of resistance-training equipment and resistance training in general. Perhaps the most important though, is the realisation that resistance training is not just the province of the body-builder (or muscle-man). Scientific research and hundreds of thousands of practical experiences have shown that resistance training can lead to all kinds of different training effects according to how the training programme is structured and it should not be thought of as simply a muscle-building activity.

For example, resistance training may be used by the sports person to great effect to improve performance. All sports activities require varying degrees of muscular strength, muscular endurance, muscular power, and aerobic and anaerobic fitness. All of these are components of physical fitness which can be enhanced with the right type of resistance-training programme. All things being equal, the performer who is the fittest will perform better and tire less easily. It has also been shown that the fitter individual is also less likely to show a deterioration in basic skills associated with his or her sport as the game/event progresses.

Further, resistance-training programmes

Fig 1  *Derek Redmond, 400m runner, one of many world class sportsmen who regularly train with weights to improve their performance.*

can be specifically designed with both the sports activity and the individual performer in mind to make the programme as relevant as possible to the activity and to the strengths and weaknesses of the person who is competing. In other words, it is quite possible to put together a programme for oarsmen which emphasises the particular demands of this sport, or an equally different and effective

7

programme for footballers, gymnasts, javelin throwers or any other sport/sports performer you care to mention. All that is necessary is an analysis of the sport carried out alongside an analysis of the performer who is training. The potential for resistance training to be both event and performer specific is certainly an important advantage that this type of training has over other training methods. For not only can muscles be conditioned in a similar (yet often more intensive) fashion to the way they will be required to function during a particular sports activity, the sports performer's individual weaknesses can be worked upon. Consequently it is quite possible to sort out for example, muscular strength imbalances which could be a limiting factor in how effectively a sports person performs certain skills or techniques associated with his or her sport, even to the extent of correcting imbalances which could or perhaps do lead to injury.

Perhaps many of the arguments for including resistance training in a sports person's training schedule are best illustrated by the remarks of British athletics coach George Gandy, who was training adviser to arguably the best 800/1,500m runner of all time, Sebastian Coe. When Coe was first analysed, Gandy's comments were:

'His arms and shoulders were very thin and lacked strength. His abdominals and back muscles were also weak and, most important of all, he lacked power in the main locomotor groups – the quadriceps and gluteals. The length of his stride already approached 6½ feet but tended to decrease noticeably as he tired and his leg cadence was not impressive. Furthermore, an imbalance between upper and lower body development was evidenced by excessive contra-rotation of the arms.'(*Running Magazine*, July/August, 1980)

One of Gandy's solutions to the problem of Coe's weaknesses as he observed them was to recommend a programme of resistance exercises to complement Coe's running programme. The rest, as they say, is history.

Yet sportsmen and women are not the only people who can gain great benefit from regular resistance training. Muscular strength, muscular endurance and aerobic fitness are all health-related components of physical fitness. In other words, an improvement in any or all of these components leads quite simply to an improvement in an individual's general health and well-being. Not only that, improvements in these components of fitness are invariably linked to improvements in the shape, appearance and posture of the exerciser. Indeed, many would argue that it is the cosmetic improvements brought about through regular resistance training which has led to this form of training being as popular as it is today with the general public. Resistance training is by far the most effective method of shaping the body, particularly when combined with an aerobic exercise programme and suitable diet.

Resistance training is also unbelievably flexible. Programmes can be designed using little or no specialist equipment. The exercises can take up more or less space according to what is available. Exercises can be done indoors or outdoors. Programmes can be performed in groups, pairs or individually. Finally, there are so many ways of changing a programme whilst still being able to achieve results, that boredom and monotony need never be a problem.

Resistance training obviously has a lot going for it. This book explains where it has come from and exactly what it is.

# THE EVOLUTION OF RESISTANCE TRAINING AND RESISTANCE-TRAINING EQUIPMENT

Legend has it that the first person to use some form of progressive resistance training in order to both improve his fitness level and to gain a competitive edge over his rivals was a wrestler in Ancient Greece by the name of Milo. The story is told that Milo was pondering how he might increase his strength as he watched a young calf in a field. The idea came to him that it might be a good idea to pick up the calf and carry it around the field on his shoulders. Milo repeated this unusual form of training every day. Since the calf was growing steadily, Milo found that each week he was carrying a heavier and heavier weight around the field and his strength and fitness was improving accordingly. Eventually the calf became a young bull and due to this progressive resistance training, Milo became unbeatable in every competition he entered.

Whether this story is true or not it is certainly a fact that the Ancient Greeks were well aware that in order to improve the condition of their musculature it was necessary to do some form of training in which the muscles were asked to do more physical work than that which they normally performed. Knowing this, competitors in early Olympic games all trained either using the resistance afforded by their own bodies, the bodies of partners, that of rocks and boulders, or in fact any object, animate or otherwise, against which they had to apply force. In other words they were resistance training.

Quite simply then, resistance training means asking the muscles to apply force to overcome some form of resistance. If the resistance that the muscles are required to overcome is of a certain magnitude and has to be overcome often enough on a regular basis, the muscles respond with an increase in either their strength, endurance, power, and so on according to how the resistance training programme has been put together (*see* also page 25).

For many years, using the resistance of partners and objects such as boulders, millstones, logs, anvils and suchlike were the only available methods of resistance training. Since such objects were very heavy in the first place and could only be lifted by very large individuals in the first instance, resistance training came to be purely associated with feats of strength performed by circus strongmen. Perhaps this was the reason that there is a long standing, yet misplaced reputation that this method of training is devoted purely to increasing size and strength. The relationship between increasing muscular size and resistance training was further established in the general public's eyes with the emergence of the sport of body-building, particularly throughout the seventies when body-building gained far more media recognition and many of the sports heroes, like eight times Mr Olympia, Arnold Schwarzenegger, became film and television stars.

It was about this time that more research began to be carried out looking at the effects of resistance training on other components of fitness as well as into how different people respond to different types of training programmes. With the growing realisation that resistance training could be used with many different training aims in mind to produce a variety of different training benefits plus an increasingly health-conscious public, resistance training for fitness began to increase in popularity. With this increasing demand, equipment manufacturers quickly realised that the traditional apparatus used for resistance training was perhaps not as user-friendly as it could be.

Body-builders, strength athletes and many sportspeople may well have been extremely happy with simple barbells, dumb-bells and

Fig 2   A simple pulley machine.

iron-weight discs of various sizes, but the more fitness-conscious exerciser originally found such basic items of equipment less than appealing. A variety of basic weight-training machines had been developed for strength athletes and body-builders in the fifties. These included various pulley machines of a plate-loading variety, which consisted of a cage or platform to which weight discs could be added and which ran up and down a frame when force was applied to the cable attached to it. Such basic resistance training machines allowed more exercises to be performed, with greater safety and also made it easier to isolate and work muscles more intensively. These basic designs were adapted to make the machines more attractive to the general user by replacing the weight platform with a weight stack. This meant that to change the weight you were using, all that you had to do was to move the

position of a selector pin in the weight stack to the desired weight for you.

At approximately the same time, equipment designers also realised that the force which a muscle can exert (and consequently the resistance it can overcome) depends upon many factors including the length of the muscle, the speed at which the muscle changes length, the joint angle as the muscle exerts force and even the characteristics of the muscle itself (*see* page 20).

To try and take some of these factors into account and make resistance training equipment more effective, designers such as Arthur Jones (the man originally behind Nautilus equipment) began to design equipment which incorporated pulleys which were not of a uniform shape. This meant that as the exercise was performed the amount of force which a muscle had to exert varied. So for example, at a joint angle where a muscle might be able to exert only a small amount of force, the machine design took this into account and the resistance to be overcome was correspondingly less than at a joint angle where a muscle could generate more force. In this way variable resistance equipment was developed, theoretically allowing a muscle or muscle group to be worked maximally throughout its whole range of movement.

Manufacturers also began to take into consideration the fact that different people are of different shapes and sizes and began to make their machines more adjustable to accommodate different limb lengths. All these modifications and several others meant that by the late seventies, resistance training equipment had evolved into highly sophisticated, simple to use, fully adjustable, comfortable single-station or multi-station units capable of being used safely by all kinds of people with many and varied training aims.

However, the story does not end there. Whilst weight stacks are the preferred method of providing resistance as far as most

*Fig 3    A typical Nautilus machine.*

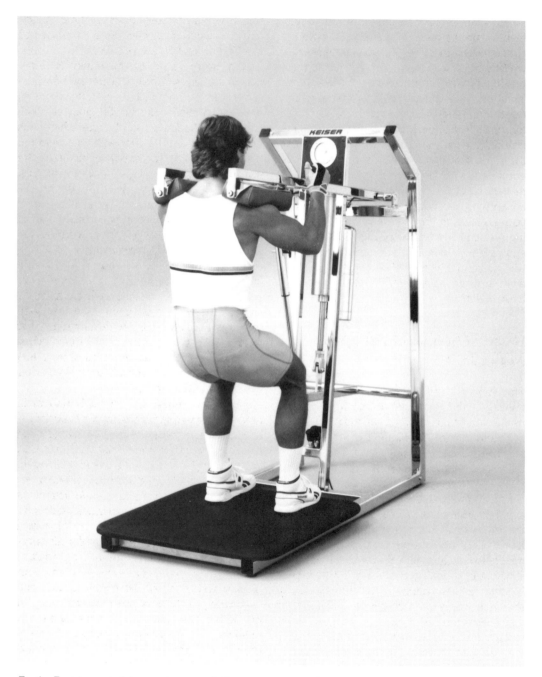

*Fig 4   Resistance-training equipment which uses compressed air as the resistance.*

manufacturers are concerned, some, equipment designers have used hydraulic cylinders containing air or oil to provide the resistance, whilst others have opted for electromagnetic braking or even motor drives. Some manufacturers have even incorporated sophisticated computer technology to allow their machines to talk back to you as you exercise. Naturally, each manufacturer tends to make the claim that their system is better or more effective than their competitors'. The truth is that all resistance training equipment has its advantages and disadvantages. Provided that you exercise according to established training principles and according to how the equipment in question should be used, you will get results whatever equipment you use, even if your equipment is only your own body-weight.

# RESISTANCE TRAINING MYTHS

The biggest myth surrounding resistance training – that this type of exercise is only useful for building massive muscles – has hopefully been dispelled. However, other reasons are also given by sportspeople and the public alike for not wanting to train in this manner.

For example, a frequently used excuse for avoiding resistance training is that it will lead the exerciser to become muscle bound – or less flexible and mobile. There is little evidence to support this view as far as well-structured, appropriate training is concerned. Indeed, regular resistance training has been shown to lead to increases in flexibility, rather than decreases. At the very least, an individual's flexibility is likely to stay the same as that enjoyed before the resistance training programme began. This myth, once again, probably arose because of the early association of resistance training and body-builders

and is worth discussing since there is one instance when a certain type of resistance training will lead to less mobility.

A person's range of movement is determined by many factors, one of which is known as the apposition of soft tissue. In other words, fleshy parts of the body can limit how much a joint angle changes when such tissues come into contact with one another. If a body-builder for example increases the size of his or her upper and lower arm muscles dramatically, then the degree of movement possible at the elbow joint will be limited by the contact of muscle against muscle when he or she tries to bend at the elbow. Assuming equally massive development throughout all of the major muscle groups of the body, the body-builder in question would certainly exhibit a more limited range of movement than someone with less marked muscular development. Yet having said that, research on weight-lifters and other strength athletes has shown that many of them are far more flexible than other sportsmen and women.

The other reason this muscle-bound myth may have arisen is related to poor resistance-training programme design. A well-balanced conditioning programme should emphasise the full range of movement and training of muscles so that imbalances in strength for example are not created to the extent of interfering with normal posture, gait and effective performance of everyday tasks and sports techniques. Well-structured resistance-training programmes should also feature adequate warming-up and warming-down phases, with each of these phases including preparatory or developmental stretching. If the above conditions are not met then it is possible to restrict normal ranges of movement through abnormal or imbalanced development. Movements of the arm at the shoulder joint may be restricted if the exerciser concentrates on work for the chest

13

*Fig 5    Marine Jahan, proving the point that resistance training does not make women less feminine.*

jump, pole vault, steeplechase or hammer event in the modern Olympic games.)

The arguments against women engaging in resistance training activities it would seem are largely cultural and social, since physiologically there is no reason why women should not be able to train as hard as men and gain the same type of training benefits, since male muscle is effectively the same as female muscle and consequently can be conditioned in the same way. For example, studies have shown that as a result of resistance training, women can gain as much strength and at the same rate as men, with some research even indicating they can achieve a greater rate of strength increase than that shown by men on the same type of programme.

Some women have fears regarding increases in muscular size but these are also unfounded. The relationship (or lack of it) between resistance training and muscle size has already been discussed and it has been pointed out that a certain type of training schedule needs to be followed if size increases are to be dramatic and then only if the exercising individual has the most appropriate body type (*see* page 28). These points are as valid for women as they are for men. In addition, some exercise physiologists would argue that whilst a woman can become much stronger as a result of appropriate resistance training, she is less likely to develop massive muscles because of hormonal differences, with a female's lack of the so-called muscle-building hormone testosterone often being put forward as the main factor in not becoming muscularly massive. Here it should also be pointed out that muscle size and strength do not always go hand in hand and a person can be immensely strong without being particularly massive, relatively speaking.

The above does not, however, mean that women cannot gain muscle size. Some women, just like some men, will have a

muscles (which brings the arm towards the mid-line of the body) without balancing out the exercise programme with exercises for those muscles of the back and shoulders which produce the opposite action.

Another myth is that resistance training is not as appropriate for women as it is for men. Again, such an argument against resistance training has largely evolved because of the association of resistance training with men and muscles, particularly in times, unlike today, when women were not regarded as being as physically able and capable of training as hard as men. To illustrate this point it is only within the last decade in athletics that women have been able to compete at Olympic level in the marathon, a race which was regarded as being too strenuous for a woman. The same is also true of the event known as the 'man-killer', namely the 400m hurdles. (Interestingly, there is still no women's triple greater potential to add muscle mass with the appropriate resistance-training programme precisely because of differences in body type, hormone levels and basic genetic make-up. Female body-builders illustrate this quite clearly and like the men at the top of this sport, as in so many other sports, become champions because they are more suited to the activity – genetically – than other competitors.

In an increasingly fashion and fitness conscious world, women are finding that there is every reason to engage in some form of resistance-training programme, rather than finding unsubstantiated arguments not to. The fitness and shaping benefits of appropriate resistance-training programmes mean that, just like men, they can achieve and maximise their body's potential.

# NEW DEVELOPMENTS

As resistance training has gained more and more support from the scientific body, some interesting new developments have occurred. For example, some exercise scientists are of the opinion that resistance training and training with weights in particular, may be a very valid method of conditioning children if undertaken with due care, attention and supervision. The American Orthopaedic Society for Sports Medicine (AOSSM), held a strength workshop in 1985 and the workshop group agreed that strength training for pre-pubescent boys and girls 'is safe with proper programme design'. Previously, resistance training and weight training especially, had been regarded as being potentially too hazardous to growing muscles, connective tissues and young bodies in general. However, it would seem that if the resistance programme emphasises exemplary techniques, avoids high resistances, is well structured and appropriately supervised by a

knowledgeable coach at all times, children will gain from this form of conditioning.

The AOSSM also pointed out that competitive lifts should be prohibited and that the resistance training should form part of 'an overall comprehensive programme designed to increase motor skills and level of fitness'. Other authorities in this field have also recommended that all children about to undertake resistance training should have a full medical examination and that in the training programme itself, difficult overhead lifts, or exercises where the spine is under high loads should be avoided.

At the other end of the spectrum, resistance training for older adults (fifty-five plus) is also gaining support, since aspects of the ageing process can be slowed down with appropriate physical conditioning. For example, it is common for muscle mass to deteriorate by as much as thirty per cent between the ages of thirty and seventy and for bone loss to be equally marked, particularly in women. With decreases in flexibility and physical work capacity and increases in blood pressure amongst other things, the older individual will naturally begin to find everyday life more demanding.

Whilst this functional decline is not preventable, regular physical activity can certainly slow down the rate of decline and resistance training can be very effective in maintaining muscle mass and bone density for as long as possible.

As with any exercise programme, prescribing exercise for the older person should begin with an accurate health and fitness (including a careful examination of muscles, joints and ranges of movement) assessment, particularly since an individual's chronological age can be quite far removed from his or her physiological age. Other than that the principles of resistance-training programming are identical to those for younger individuals. It should be noted, however, that rate of

15

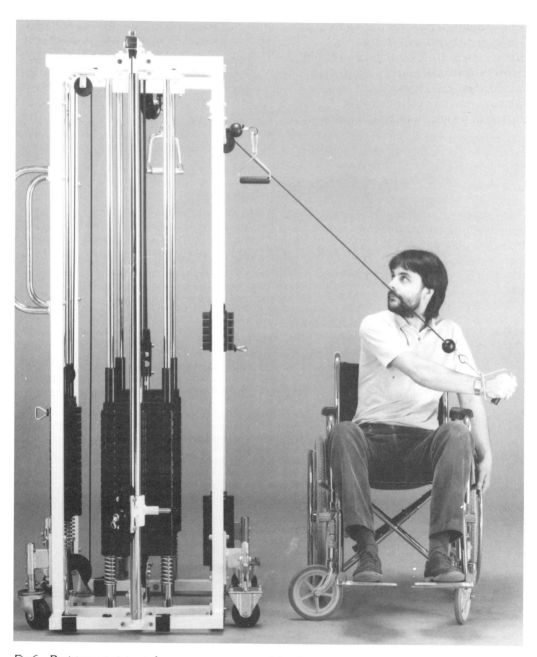

*Fig 6    Resistance training is for everyone – young, old and disabled.*

improvement tends to be slower with advancing age and that to avoid potentially harmful rises in blood pressure, high-intensity resistance training should be avoided. (*See* also pages 22–4)

Finally, other developments in the prescription of resistance training have included programmes to be carried out ante- and post-natally and other programmes have been very effective in improving the fitness levels of post-operative cardiac patients. Bearing all the above information in mind the flexibility of resistance training is truly beyond question.

# 1   Understanding Muscle

To understand just how and why different resistance training systems and programmes produce different training effects and results it is necessary to first understand some basic facts regarding the anatomy and physiology of muscle.

Muscle is commonly placed in three categories according to location and type. The three categories are cardiac muscle (the heart), visceral muscle (which is that found in the walls of hollow internal structures such as arteries) and skeletal muscle which includes all those muscles which are attached to the bones of the skeleton.

Resistance training programmes are predominantly concerned with skeletal muscle (cardio-vascular changes associated with resistance training are discussed on pages 21–4) and the easiest way to understand skeletal muscle is to look at how it is structured.

A typical skeletal muscle is covered in strong connective tissue. If this muscle is cut across the middle (*see Fig 7*) it is possible to appreciate that skeletal muscle is composed of bundles of muscle fibres (or cells) bound together by more connective tissue. Also obvious is the fact the muscle contains varying amounts of fat and is richly supplied with blood vessels as well as nerves.

Using a microscope it is possible to look at an individual muscle fibre and see that it is basically long in structure, has an obvious cell wall and contains fluid and various other structures, including hundreds of very fine, threadlike strands of protein, arranged in parallel which are called myofibrils. A closer look at an individual myofibril further reveals

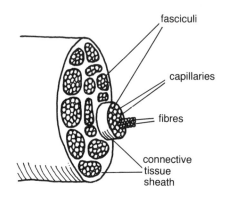

Fig 7   *A section through a skeletal muscle.*

that it too is very ordered in its structure and is made up of a careful arrangement of thick and thin proteins known as actin and myosin.

The process by which muscle contracts or develops force is best described by what is known as the sliding filament theory. According to this theory, when a nerve impulse reaches a muscle cell, electrical and chemical changes cause one set of proteins to slide past the other. The end result of actin and myosin sliding past one another is a shortening of the myofibril. As each myofibril shortens

18

at the same time (having received the same nerve impulse) the entire muscle cell effectively shortens.

The nerve impulse does not just reach one nerve cell at a time. Motor nerves (those carrying impulses to muscles and glands) serve many muscle cells, particularly in a large muscle. For example, one motor nerve in the quadriceps muscle at the front of the thigh may innervate a few thousand individual muscle cells. A motor nerve and all the muscle cells it is connected with is known as a motor unit. More or less motor units will be involved in overcoming resistance according to how great that resistance is. If the resistance is very great as many motor units as possible will be involved in the production of force and vice versa. This arrangement of muscle cells and nerves into functional units allows for varying amounts of force to be generated to cope with the varying resistances different activities require.

However, not all muscle cells are the same. It is possible to consider different types of muscle cell according to how they contract, or twitch, when they receive a stimulus. Using this method of classification, there are two basic types of muscle fibre: fast twitch (FT) and slow twitch (ST). Generally speaking, FT fibres are better suited to very rapid, forceful contractions, whilst ST fibres are better suited for slower, more prolonged activity. FT fibres tend to tire easily, whilst ST fibres are more energy efficient and resistant to fatigue. Due to this FT fibres are found in abundance in sprinters, whilst ST fibres are associated in quantity with distance runners.

Fast twitch fibres can also be sub-divided further into two main types, known as type IIa and type IIb (in which case ST fibres may be referred to as type I). This is because types IIa and IIb have some quite recognisable differences. IIa fibres are more fatigue resistant than IIb fibres and have a greater capillary network to supply them with blood. In this

respect they are more like type I fibres.

The ratio of type I and type II fibres is determined by heredity. Of interest, however, is the fact that different types of training can lead to fibres becoming more like one another. Type IIb fibres may well increase the number of mitochondria (the cell's energy power houses) they possess by endurance training and in so doing may effectively 'become' type IIa fibres.

# DEVELOPING FORCE AND OVERCOMING RESISTANCE

The above information explains how muscle can contract or develop force, but it does not explain how movement occurs and how resistance is overcome. Effectively the structure of muscle is such that the result of a nerve impulse is a muscle fibre attempting to bring its ends together. Because muscle cells are bound together by connective tissue, the contraction of muscle is applied through the connective tissue. The connective tissue which extends continuously throughout muscle eventually joins together to form a strong cord or a broad flat sheet. The cord of connective tissue is known as a tendon, whilst the sheet of tissue is called an aponeurosis. Force generated by muscle cells is effectively applied to bones or other muscles via these structures. Because bones meet at joints and joints (according to their structure) allow more or less movement, the end result of muscles contracting is movement itself.

Whilst a muscle essentially just tries to bring its ends together, sometimes it does not always succeed. Sometimes, too, it brings its ends together at specific speeds. These facts allow different types of muscular contractions to be discussed. So, if a muscle succeeds in overcoming resistance and shortens to bring its ends together, this is known as a concentric contraction. A muscle can also overcome resistance whilst maintaining its length, in which case the muscle is said to be engaging in a static (or isometric) contraction. Muscles can also lengthen whilst developing force, with this type of force development being known as an eccentric contraction. Finally, if a muscle develops force and the rate of change of joint angle is constant, this is known as an isokinetic contraction.

Many people whilst training may well come across the terms negative and positive work. These are just popular phrases for eccentric (negative) and concentric (positive) contractions. All muscles regularly engage in concentric, static and eccentric contractions and will do so according to the movement they are performing. Controlled isokinetic contractions and isokinetic training, however, require sophisticated training equipment, such as Cybex.

## Factors Affecting Force Development

Several factors which determine how much force muscles can develop and how much resistance can be overcome have already been mentioned, both in this chapter and in the preceding introduction. These include the size and density of a muscle and its fibre type composition. Other factors which are important include the joint angle at which the muscle exerts force, the length of muscle and the rate or speed of contraction.

Muscles tend to produce greater force at greater lengths, although if this means that the muscle finds itself developing tension at an ineffective joint angle for the application of force, the amount of resistance which can be overcome will not be great. Equally important, muscles are capable of developing more force at slow speeds and as speed of contraction increases, the amount of force

decreases. The relevance of these facts to training is discussed on pages 38–9.

It has also been shown that it is possible to generate more force during eccentric contractions and when a strong eccentric contraction is followed by a rapid concentric contraction (as in depth jumping). Again, the implications of this information as far as training is concerned is discussed on pages 38–9.

Finally, simple factors affect force development. Muscles can generate more force when they are warm – hence the importance of warming up thoroughly prior to training or competition. Individuals can also be hypnotised to persuade them to generate more force. Since hypnosis can lead to quite marked differences in overcoming resistances, strong psychological influences must be at work inhibiting the production of force. A warm-up phase should perhaps also be geared to getting yourself into the right frame of mind (psyching yourself up). And if you think that the shouts made by some individuals whilst training may be excessive, bear in mind that some researchers have been able to demonstrate improvements in resistances overcome when subjects shouted as they performed an exercise compared to when they did not!

## Energy for Muscular Contraction

In order for actin and myosin to slide past one another, energy must be supplied. Muscle cells, like all the cells in the body, can only work using a specific type of energy which is provided when a compound (stored in cells and known as ATP) breaks down. ATP (adenosine triphosphate) is a high-energy compound, meaning that when it does break down, significant amounts of energy are released and it is this energy which powers the cell. However, the ATP molecule having been broken down to release its energy, has been likened to a battery which has run down and must now be recharged in order for it to be able to fuel the cell's activity again. The energy for recharging ATP comes either from the breakdown of another high energy compound, phosphocreatine or PC (also stored within cells) or from energy released from the breakdown of foods.

The simplest method of recharging the ATP battery is to use the energy from the breakdown of PC. Since PC is stored within the cell and no lengthy chemical reactions are involved, this system of energy production (often referred to as the ATP–PC system) provides energy for muscular contractions that occur rapidly, yet whose total time is short-lived as in strength training using say one set of six repetitions (*see* pages 33–5). More energy can be provided to recharge the ATP battery using the energy released from food. Carbohydrates can be stored within muscles as well as in the liver and will also be circulating in the blood as blood glucose. These carbohydrates can be broken down in two ways to provide energy: firstly in the presence and secondly in the absence of oxygen. If oxygen is not present at the muscle cell (specifically in the mitochondria) carbohydrates will be broken down incompletely to release limited amounts of energy. At the same time a by-product, known as lactic acid will be produced. This incomplete breakdown of carbohydrate is known as anaerobic glycolysis and lactic acid is the substance which, when it accumulates in muscles, is responsible for that tingling, burning feeling, which is often experienced during exercises which involve less than maximal effort but which involve many repetitions (twenty plus).

When oxygen is present at the cellular level, carbohydrates can be broken down completely to release far more energy than if they are broken down incompletely and no

lactic acid is formed. The process is then known as aerobic glycolysis. Fats can also be broken down aerobically (they cannot be broken down anaerobically) yet oxygen is needed at the cellular level in considerable quantity and many lengthy, sequential, chemical reactions are necessary.

The specific system which is used to provide energy for muscular contraction depends upon the intensity and duration of the training or physical activity in question. The general rule is 'the more intense the activity, the shorter its duration and the more emphasis that is placed upon the quickest, most immediate methods of energy production. High intensity strength training for example, will emphasise the ATP–PC system; less intense muscular endurance work will look more to anaerobic glycolysis.

Worth noting, however, is the fact that depleted fuel stores can be replenished relatively quickly, yet replenishment depends upon the fuel supply and how exhausted the fuel supply in question has become. Fuel stores for short (fifteen second) intense bouts of activity can be replenished almost completely in about the same time period (fifteen to twenty seconds). Longer bouts of activity obviously lead to greater fuel store depletion, hence replenishment takes longer. With continuous physical activity which lasts longer than seventy minutes or so, it is quite possible to exhaust supplies of glycogen (carbohydrate) which may take several days to replenish.

# THE CARDIO-VASCULAR SYSTEM

Whilst the preceding information regarding how muscle develops force and where muscles get their energy from give most of the information which is necessary in order to appreciate resistance-training programme design, some information about the cardio-vascular system is perhaps also of value to the understanding of planned exercise.

Briefly, the cardio-vascular system consists of the blood, the heart and the blood vessels. This system has numerous functions including the distribution of oxygen and nutrients to the cells of the body; the carriage of carbon dioxide and other waste products away from the cells; the maintenance of the correct acid/alkali balance of the body; protection against disease; prevention of haemorrhage; and the regulation of body temperature.

At the centre of the system is the heart – a pump which maintains the circulation of blood around the body. Essentially, the heart is a hollow, muscular organ about the size of a man's clenched fist, which is divided into four chambers. The upper chambers are known as atria, whilst the lower chambers are known as ventricles.

Blood vessels carrying blood away from the heart are called arteries and have strong, elastic, muscular walls. These become smaller and smaller as they spread throughout the body, eventually becoming small arteries known as arterioles, before becoming thin-walled vessels called capillaries. Capillaries are found in quantity in muscle, organised into extensive networks known as capillary beds. The entrance of blood into capillary beds is controlled through the presence of rings of muscle called pre-capillary sphincters. It is at the capillary level that the exchange of gases (oxygen and carbon dioxide) and nutrients takes place. Blood which returns to the heart is carried by veins which have thinner, less muscular walls than arteries and also feature one-way valves to prevent the blood flowing back. The largest veins in the body are known as the inferior and superior vena cavae.

The different blood vessels and the heart constitute a closed system of tubes with blood being pumped round in one direction.

This is best illustrated by considering the path that blood follows upon entering the right atrium, having been delivered to this collecting chamber of the heart via the superior and inferior vena cavae. As the right atrium fills, the blood passes through a one-way valve into the right ventricle. This chamber fills, the blood is then ejected via a forceful contraction through the pulmonary artery and carried off to the lungs. Here the exchange of gases occurs (carbon dioxide is unloaded, whilst oxygen is taken on board) and the oxygen-rich, carbon dioxide deficient blood is returned to the left atrium via the pulmonary veins. The blood then passes through another one-way valve, before entering the muscular, left ventricle which sends the blood off through the aorta and round the whole system again.

On average, the heart beats at rest around seventy times per minute. With each beat the left ventricle ejects an amount of blood (the stroke volume). At rest the typical stroke volume of an untrained person is approximately 70ml. Consequently, in one minute the amount of blood circulating through the cardio-vascular system is seventy beats multiplied by 70ml, which is approximately five litres. The volume of blood ejected from the left ventricle in one minute is known as the cardiac output.

In many ways, the heart can be thought of as being a pressure generating machine, in that through its regular contractions it generates pressure which forces blood through the blood vessels. Blood pressure is thus the term which is used to describe the force exerted upon the walls of blood vessels. Naturally this varies according (amongst other things) to whether the heart is contracting or not. When the heart contracts, the pressure exerted by blood upon blood vessel walls is obviously greater than the pressure exerted upon the same blood vessel walls when the ventricles are filling up. When a

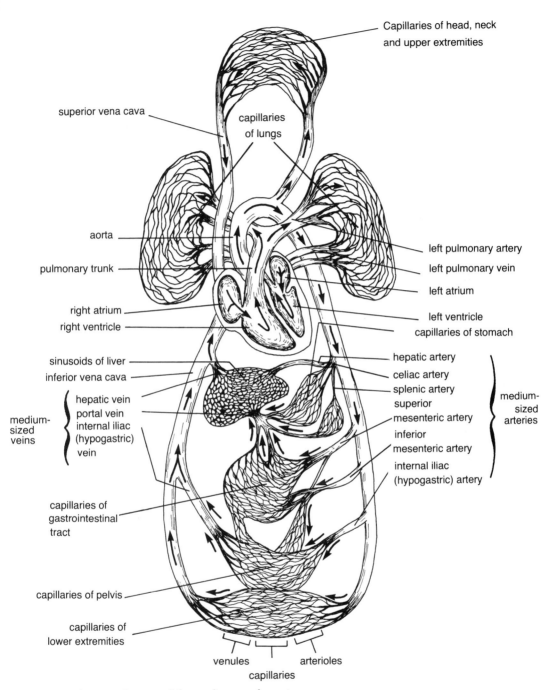

Capillaries of head, neck and upper extremities

superior vena cava

capillaries of lungs

aorta

pulmonary trunk

right atrium

right ventricle

left pulmonary artery

left pulmonary vein

left atrium

left ventricle

capillaries of stomach

sinusoids of liver

inferior vena cava

medium-sized veins

hepatic vein

portal vein

internal iliac (hypogastric) vein

hepatic artery

celiac artery

splenic artery

superior mesenteric artery

inferior mesenteric artery

internal iliac (hypogastric) artery

medium-sized arteries

capillaries of gastrointestinal tract

capillaries of pelvis

capillaries of lower extremities

venules          arterioles

capillaries

*Fig 8    A schematic diagram of the cardio-vascular system.*

person's blood pressure is taken, the two figures which are given (the average values being 120/80mmHg) reflect this.

Yet this value is an average, resting value for healthy individuals. All kinds of factors can affect blood pressure and it is worth while mentioning one of them – muscular contraction – at this point. Blood vessels have to run through and around muscles in order that the muscles and other tissues can receive an adequate blood supply. When a muscle contracts forcefully, the blood vessels are effectively 'squashed' and the more forceful the muscular contraction, the more the passage of blood through the vessel is restricted. In regular, rhythmical contractions of muscle this is not a problem since the time during which blood flow is restricted is very short. However, if the contraction is forceful and sustained, as in a static contraction, blood flow is severely restricted and blood pressure consequently increases as the body attempts to pump blood into what is now a region of high pressure. Regions of high pressure in the body can also be caused by holding one's breath – the chest and abdominal cavity assume a relatively high pressure, preventing the return of blood at low pressure (in the veins) to the heart.

Such increases in blood pressure brought about by sustained static contractions or through holding your breath may prove hazardous for individuals who already have a problem with high blood pressure in the first instance and so should be avoided. Even in healthy individuals, the restriction of normal blood flow brought about through these practices may lead to feelings of nausea and dizziness. It is also believed that it is the increase in heart rate – in order to increase blood pressure – during sustained muscular contractions (particularly involving the arms above head-height) which leads to greater blood pressure increases. This is because of the extra work that the heart has to do

pumping blood vertically against the force of gravity and it leads to the problems encountered in trying to use heart rate methods for assessing exercise intensity whilst resistance training.

During traditional aerobic exercise activities, such as running, the harder an individual works the greater the demand for oxygen by the working muscles and the greater the heart rate. It has been shown that during continuous aerobic exercise the increase in oxygen consumption is mirrored by the increase in heart rate, enabling exercise intensity to be gauged with accuracy simply by monitoring one's pulse. However, this does not seem to be the case with resistance training where high heart rates may be equally indicative of an increased blood pressure as the cardio-vascular system attempts to pump blood into and through regions of high pressure in the body.

# BASIC RESPONSES TO TRAINING – TRAINING THEORY

The basic anatomy and physiology contained within this chapter gives an insight into how the body (specifically muscle and the cardio-vascular system) is put together and how it functions. However, little has been said so far with regard to how the body responds and adapts to exercise and training, other than to state, as in the Introduction, the many different benefits associated with different types of training schedules. Whilst the adaptations to different types of training are listed fully in the various sections of this book dealing with each type of training, it is perhaps worth while to briefly indicate just why such adaptations are likely to occur.

Many textbooks dealing with the subjects of anatomy and physiology use the motor car as an example of how the body works: fuel = food; motor = muscles, and so on, yet this analogy can be very misleading when it comes to discussing exercise physiology. If you drive a motor car every day it will gradually wear down and eventually need replacing – the Automobile Association has estimated that the useful life of a well-kept automobile is only around eight years. But if you keep your body physically active not only does it not wear out as quickly, it actually becomes more efficient and less likely to break down, enabling you to enjoy a useful life ten times that of your car!

Physical activity and regular exercise, quite simply, improve the basic functioning of the body. If you give muscles appropriate strength training to do they become stronger and if you give the whole body aerobic exercise to do, the efficiency of the cardio-vascular system improves – these are only two examples of how the efficiency of the body improves with use.

The reason such beneficial adaptations to exercise and training occur can be looked at in very basic 'survival' terms. When the body is asked to perform any specific type of exercise, it looks for the best method of performing that activity, with the best method being that which poses the least possible stress on the various systems of the body involved in that activity. If we take strength training and ask a muscle or muscle group to develop high forces it does so. If this high force development is repeated often enough over a period of time, with adequate recovery periods between the work bouts several adaptations occur. Initially the muscle and muscles which are asked to develop the force get better at overcoming resistance by involving more muscle fibres at the right time (in other words skill level improves). Such skill-related adaptations to training occur throughout the first two to three weeks of a resistance-training programme and largely explain why it is common for individuals to find themselves lifting considerably greater weights in an exercise compared to when they started, even though there have been no observable changes within the muscles themselves.

Then, provided the muscle or muscles are still being asked to exert high forces, changes within the muscle cells themselves occur as the training programme progresses. For example, the amount of contractile protein within individual muscle cells increases, making them more dense and/or increasing the cell's cross-sectional area. Other changes will occur too, including changes in the strength of other exercise-stressed connective tissues, such as within tendons, ligaments and bone. All of these adaptive changes occur as a result of the stress of exercise, with the body adapting so that the exercise or physical activity is no longer as demanding – and hence as hazardous – as it was previously.

Observations such as these and others dealing with the effects of different training programmes on the body have led to the foundation of what is often called *training theory*. Training theory essentially outlines the many variables which can be manipulated in order to achieve the desired training effect. Again, these variables are discussed fully in the appropriate section of this book. To give an overview, however, the main training variables which need to be considered when designing a programme are the type of exercise, its intensity, its duration and its frequency. Other factors which will influence how an individual responds will further include specific characteristics associated with that individual, including their trainability, along with their general state of health, as well as the appropriateness of recovery and rest intervals between training or exercise bouts.

Finally it should also be appreciated that all training effects are reversible. In other words, if you are no longer carrying out the same type of physical activity which led to the training effects you enjoyed up until recently, a gradual decline in your physical prowess is to be expected. No hard and fast rules have been established regarding detraining, yet it seems to be the case that the longer you have spent achieving a pinnacle of fitness, the more gradual is the decline. It would also appear that having reached a level of fitness, strength and so on with which you are satisfied, that level of physical prowess can be maintained on less training than was spent achieving it.

# 2  Self-Assessment and Training Aims Analysis

In order to put together a training programme which is going to produce the desired training effects, not only do you have to structure your programme according to recognised training principles (as outlined in each training section) you also have to correctly assess your initial fitness level and training aim.

The assessment of your training aim is perhaps the simplest of these two tasks to perform. All you really have to do is ask yourself the question 'what do I want to achieve from my training programme?' It may be that you want to achieve an improvement in general or specific fitness or improve muscular strength, endurance or power. You may, on the other hand, wish to increase the size of your muscles, or just tone them up. There are obviously many options. For easy access to all the relevant information regarding your training aim, each component of fitness, or training aim that you may have, has its own distinct programming/training section. You should refer to the appropriate section for in-depth training information. *Fig 9* given here lists the various training sections and indicates on which pages each section can be found.

The next task is perhaps more time-consuming, although not difficult. In order to see change or improvement in any aspect of fitness or shape that you may be emphasising in your training programme you need to have a reference point. That reference point is your initial fitness level. In each training section you will find a simple test or assessment

| Aim | Pages |
| --- | --- |
| Resistance training for improved muscular strength | 31–5 |
| Resistance training for increased muscular size | 35–7 |
| Resistance training for improved muscular power | 37-9 |
| Resistance training for improved muscular endurance | 39–42 |
| Resistance training for improved aerobic fitness | 42–5 |
| Resistance training to shape your body | 45–7 |
| Resistance training for improved sports performance | 47–8 |

*Fig 9   Training aims table.*

procedure for the training aim in question. You should perform this test before beginning any training programme (a combination training programme may require several different tests) and see how you fare. After a suitable period of training (as indicated in each training section) the test or assessment procedure should be repeated. The differences in your scores on the subsequent tests compared with your initial score will be evidence of the achievement of your training aims. Further, such assessments repeated on a regular basis will show your continued improvement as a result of following your training programme – effectively acting as a motivational tool. To make sure you monitor these improvements, keep a training diary. At the beginning of the diary, write the date and any measurements/assessments you are advised to take in each training section. You should then log your training each week as indicated. Reassessments of fitness or shape should also be dated and noted. You can then see how effective the weeks of training have been in producing improvement between assessments. The fact that you have also written down your training accurately from week to week enables you to see what type of training has been most – or least – successful for you. This information is consequently extremely useful in deciding whether it is necessary to adapt or progress your programme and if so, how you should proceed.

In all the training programmes given later in the text, it is necessary to be realistic. Whilst everyone will achieve improvement whatever their training aim if they follow the recommendations and guide-lines given in this book, the rate of improvement will differ from individual to individual. This difference in trainability is largely genetically determined and is therefore influenced by your body type as well as by your determination and how much work and effort you are prepared to invest in order to achieve your goal.

This first point is perhaps one of the most crucial when it comes to determining the extent of the training effects you are likely to experience when following a progressive resistance training programme. Put simply, all training effects are basically superimposed upon the body you begin with. In other words, your body is the foundation upon which you build your fitness and shape. Some people naturally have bodies which are better suited to adapt to certain types of

training. Taking the effect of training for improved muscular size on different body types, firstly it should be explained that there are various ways of classifying body types, with the most common method being that known as somatotyping. According to this method the different characteristics that individuals possess allow them to be broadly separated into three main body types: *endomorph*, *mesomorph*, or *ectomorph*. A person who is predominantly endomorphic naturally has a greater fat mass than the other two types and is popularly described as being 'round'. A predominantly mesomorphic individual on the other hand tends to be square, stocky and muscular, whilst the predominantly ectomorphic person tends to be very lean, angular and linear. Few individuals exist at the extreme of each division, the majority of people exhibit characteristics which are a combination of body types. So, it is common to find endomorphic-mesomorphs, for example, or mesomorphic-ectomorphs (although no endomorphic-ectomorphs).

When training for muscular size it is the more muscular body type in the first instance (the mesomorph) who tends to show great gains in muscularity, with the more ectomorphic individual showing the least gains. This does not mean that the person with high ectomorphic characteristics does not show improvements in size, only that they are less marked (an ectomorph has virtually no chance of 'bulking up' to become bodybuilding's Mr Universe). Similarly, the more endomorphic individual will always have a problem in trying to become lean, he/she is naturally meant to carry more fat mass than the typically thin ectomorph. This does not however mean that they should be fat, only that they will never achieve the degree of lean-ness which the ectomorph exhibits naturally.

It is basic facts such as these which should be borne in mind when training – bodies are

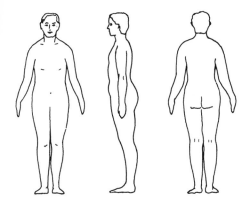

*Fig 10(a)   An endomorphic figure.*

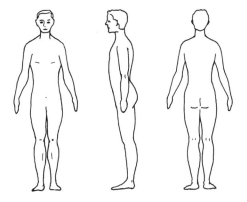

*Fig 10(b)   A mesomorphic figure.*

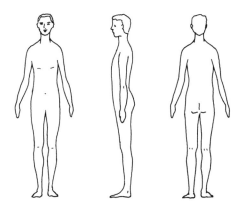

*Fig 10(c)   An ectomorphic figure.*

different and respond differently to the same type of training. And just as bodies are different in terms of shape, so they also differ in terms of their physiology. It has already been mentioned that the ratio of fast twitch and slow twitch fibres differ from individual to individual, again in a manner which is determined genetically. FT fibres are needed in quantity for activities like sprinting, whilst the more fatigue-resistant ST fibres are better suited to long distance running. Knowing this, it is no surprise that top-class sprinters invariably have a high percentage of FT fibres in their muscles whilst élite distance runners have a correspondingly high percentage of ST fibres. The favourable fibre-type ratios which each group has does not make them successful performers, however, it simply means that they are better suited for their individual activities in the first place. It is such a genetic predisposition, plus the right type of training, hard work and the will to win that then makes the champion performer.

Other physiological as well as anatomical differences also exist which lead individuals to respond differently to training, even though they are following the same rules. Such differences should be viewed for what they are, namely differences and should not be viewed negatively as problem areas. Accept your limitations and exercise around them.

Finally, you have got to want to train and put in the work if you want to see improvement. Many people may well have been brought up on the maxim, 'no pain, no gain', forget this. Instead, start thinking in terms of 'no work, no gain'. Ultimately, you will see improvements in any component of fitness or shape at a rate governed by your genetics (as discussed) and the amount of work you put in. The more work or exercise you perform (if it is of the right type, duration, intensity and frequency) the greater the improvement you will observe. However, there will come a

---

These questions are designed to assess your suitability for exercise. Please answer each question as accurately as possible, reading each question carefully.

|  |  | YES | NO |
|---|---|:---:|:---:|
| 1. | Have you ever suffered from heart disease, high blood pressure or any other cardio-vascular problem? | ☐ | ☐ |
| 2. | Is there any history of heart disease in your family? | ☐ | ☐ |
| 3. | Have you ever been troubled by accountable or unaccountable chest pain, or tightness in the chest, especially if associated with minimal effort? | ☐ | ☐ |
| 4. | Are you prone to headaches, fainting or dizziness? | ☐ | ☐ |
| 5. | Have you any medical condition which you think might interfere with your participation in an exercise programme? | ☐ | ☐ |
| 6. | Do you suffer from pain or limited movement in any joint? | ☐ | ☐ |
| 7. | Are you taking any drugs or medication at the moment, or recovering from a recent illness or operation? | ☐ | ☐ |
| 8. | Are you extremely overweight, or extremely underweight? | ☐ | ☐ |
| 9. | Are you pregnant? | ☐ | ☐ |
| 10. | Are you a newcomer to exercise and aged over 35? | ☐ | ☐ |

*Fig 11   Pre-exercise questionnaire.*

time when to see further improvement you may well have to spend a disproportionate amount of time training. If you can justify this to yourself, fine, if not be content with being almost at your peak and maintain this level of fitness/shape without investing all of your time and effort into the pursuit of excellence.

The preceding information can be summarised in one sentence 'when training, aim to maximise your potential!'

# PRE-EXERCISE ASSESSMENT

One simple test which should be carried out by anyone contemplating an exercise or training programme of any description is a pre-exercise assessment. Essentially such a test assesses your suitability for exercise. The above questionnaire does this very simply. All you have to do is read the above questions carefully, answering either yes or no to each question. If you answer no to all of the questions, rest assured that you can follow any well-structured training programme in safety. Any yes answers simply mean that you may need more specialist advice from an exercise instructor, sports coach or general practitioner before proceeding with your training.

# 3 Training Programmes

This chapter is divided into different sections, with each section dealing directly with one specific training aim. Before referring to the section dealing with the training aim which is of interest to you, it is worthwhile familiarising yourself with the following terms which are used in all the training programmes given in this chapter.

**Repetition** – the single performance of an exercise, from the start to finish position.

**Set** – the performance of a given number of repetitions of an exercise, one after the other. For example, one set of twelve repetitions, often written 1 x 12.

**Load** – the resistance which is overcome during the performance of an exercise. If referring to a 100kg barbell, the load is 100kg. If twelve repetitions of the exercise are performed, then the load (resistance) overcome in one set is 12 x 100kg = 1,200kg. If three sets of this exercise are performed then the total load for that exercise is 3 x 1,200kg = 3,600kg. Such computations are often useful when comparing the total load overcome in one exercise or in one training session.

**Recovery** – the period between sets of an exercise or between different exercises. The recovery can be rest, in which case no activity is undertaken, or it can be active, in which case some form of physical activity is performed. In both instances the recovery phase is given either in seconds or minutes.

**Positive work** – the concentric phase of an exercise (*see* also page 20).

**Negative work** – the eccentric phase of an exercise (*see* also page 20).

**Warm up** – a period of physical activity geared to safely preparing the body for more strenuous activity (*see* also pages 48–56).

**Stimulus phase** – the training period of an exercise session following the warm up.

**Warm down** – a period of physical activity geared to safely returning the body to normal following the stimulus phase.

**Preparatory stretching** – stretching exercises which are part of the warm-up phase and which are designed to take muscles and joints through their current range of movement, thus helping to avoid injury.

**Developmental stretching** – stretching exercises which are part of the warm-down phase and which are designed to increase range of movement and help prevent muscle stiffness and soreness following exercise or training.

All exercises given in the training programmes are fully illustrated and described in Chapters 4 and 5.

## RESISTANCE TRAINING FOR IMPROVED MUSCULAR STRENGTH

Maximum muscular strength is often defined as being the greatest amount of force that a muscle or muscle group can produce in a single, maximal, voluntary contraction. Muscular strength is one of the five health-related components of physical fitness (along with cardio-respiratory endurance, muscular endurance, flexibility and body composition) and possessing a high level of muscular strength allows you to lift, move and carry objects, including yourself, with relative ease. Muscular strength is also very important in sports performance, as well as being necessary for good posture. (*See* Chapter 1.)

There are various types of muscle contraction and so it is possible to speak of the maximum isometric strength of a muscle or its maximum concentric or eccentric strength. It is also possible to discuss the relative strength of an individual by comparing resistances overcome and body-weights.

Generally speaking, the strength of a muscle is closely related to its cross-sectional area, yet other factors are also important when it comes to overcoming resistance (*see* page 20). Changes which are associated with regular strength training include:

1. Muscular hypertrophy (size increase). Muscles may increase in size as a result of strength-training programmes, although this will depend upon the individual and the type of training as indicated earlier in Chapter 2. Increases in muscular size that do occur are brought about through a combination of adaptations, including an increase in the diameter of individual muscle fibres due to an increased number and size of myofibrils and contractile protein in general, and increased amounts (hence strength) of tendinous connective tissue. Increases in size may also reflect increases in the total number of capillaries in the muscle (although this is more associated with endurance training). There is also some evidence for longitudinal fibre splitting as a result of extremely intense exercise, leading some researchers to believe that the total number of muscle fibres in a muscle may – in some rare instances – increase.

2. The strength of bones, ligaments and joint structures in general increases, although only if the bones, ligaments and joints are stressed appropriately as part of the exercise/training programme.

3. The concentration of ATP, PC and glycogen stored in muscles increases and other changes also occur making it easier for muscle to generate high forces. If the strength training emphasises speed of contraction, biochemical changes which allow muscles to generate high forces very rapidly also occur.

4. Neuromuscular adaptations occur which enable muscle to involve more motor units at the right time in an exercise, allowing more resistance to be overcome.

## Assessing Muscular Strength

There are a number of ways of assessing muscular strength. In the laboratory setting it is common to use some form of strength gauge known as a dynamometer, either of the hand-grip or leg-and-back variety. In the gym (or home) environment it is easier to look at any exercise and ascertain the maximum possible resistance that can be overcome. This is done by taking an exercise – choosing one involving weight-training apparatus makes the task simpler. The exercise should then be standardised by always performing it in exactly the same way. Start with a weight which you know is not maximal and perform several repetitions of the exercise by way of warming up. After a full recovery (approximately five minutes) add more weight to the bar/weight stack and perform the exercise again. Fewer repetitions will now be possible. Repeat the process, as before, gradually adding more weight until only one repetition of the exercise can be performed. This is your maximum and is known as 1RM and reflects your strength (as well as your ability to carry out the exercise in question). With practice and experience arriving at your 1RM weight for all exercises becomes much less time-consuming and involves less trial-and-error than in the first assessment. Calculating your 1RM can be very useful in assessing the effectiveness of your training programme, as well as being of value in designing certain strength-training schedules.

# Strength-Training Systems

There are a number of different strength-training systems, yet all of them are variations along the same basic theme, in that every system requires the exerciser to exert near-maximum or even maximum force during an exercise. This is obviously a prerequisite for strength gains, bearing in mind the definition of strength given earlier.

The simplest strength-training systems often just involve the performance of one set of between eight and ten repetitions on each exercise. Note that it should only be possible to carry out the stated number of repetitions (any more and the system is not producing the right stimulus for strength gains since the force production is too low, any fewer and the total amount of work performed is again too small for strength improvement). Each repetition should be smooth and controlled, taking between four and six seconds to perform. These single-set systems invariably involve different exercises for the major muscle groups of the body and will produce strength gains in beginners. However, once an individual has reached a certain level of strength through training, then the amount of work which must be performed in order to experience further strength gains must be increased. This can be done in several ways. The most obvious way is to increase the resistance which is being overcome with each repetition. This should be done when it becomes relatively easy to perform more than the stated number of repetitions in each set. If this is happening, remember the golden rule 'never sacrifice exercise technique just to overcome greater resistance or to perform more repetitions'. Another method

of increasing the total work performed and consequently increasing the stimulus for strength gains is to increase the number of sets performed on each exercise. Multiple-set systems often involve the performance of between three and six sets of the same exercise, with each set being separated by a short rest and recovery period of between ninety seconds and five minutes, with the longer recovery period being found in strength-training systems which emphasise near maximal contractions such that as few as four repetitions of an exercise can be performed. In practice, most individuals training for strength work in pairs with a training partner. The time taken for one partner to prepare for and then to execute the exercise is often an adequate recovery period for that person. When training for pure strength, the emphasis must be on quality, hence you should allow yourself ninety seconds at least between sets.

When it comes to deciding how many sets to do, consider the total amount of work that is being performed. If you are performing three sets of ten repetitions of an exercise using a particular resistance, how does this compare to performing the same exercise with a higher resistance, for four sets of six reps? If the total work performed is less (estimated by multiplying resistance by reps by sets) then the training stimulus has been reduced.

Various multiple-set systems also exist which are designed with a high total work load in mind. One of the most effective and popular is known as a pyramid system. In pyramid training an exercise is chosen and one set of fifteen repetitions is performed. After a rest and recovery period of ninety seconds, another set of the exercise is performed, this time with a heavier weight such that only twelve repetitions can be performed. Another rest and recovery period follows, then another set, again with a heavier weight such that only ten reps can be carried out. The weight is increased again, this time the aim is to perform eight reps. This process is repeated, working through six, then four reps, until it is only possible to perform one or two reps with a weight which is, by definition, maximal. The exerciser, having gone up the pyramid is then left with the choice of carrying out the training in reverse and coming down the pyramid. As can be imagined, pyramid training requires a tremendous amount of work to be performed and it is this fact, plus the high resistance which is emphasised towards the top of the pyramid which makes this type of training so successful.

Pyramid systems can be put together in a variety of ways, choosing any descending series of numbers you wish. It is also possible to opt for either just up the pyramid or down versions, which are sometimes referred to as 'light to heavy' and 'heavy to light' systems respectively.

No mention has yet been made of the sequence or order of any exercises that may be performed in a training session. Generally it is common to perform those exercises which involve the largest muscle groups first in strength-training programmes. This is because if exercises which involve smaller muscles are employed first, the exhausted small muscles will make the performance of a large muscle group exercise more technically difficult since the fatigued small muscles cannot help the body maintain the correct exercise position or effectively aid the performance of the exercise. Because of this, it is difficult to stress the large muscles as appropriately as is necessary for strength gains.

When it comes to performing multiple-set systems, particularly those involving a pyramid, then it also becomes difficult to effectively perform more than three or four exercises, both because of the length of time such systems take and because of general fatigue. In view of this, many strength athletes will split their training so that one or possibly two body parts are performed in one training session. The following training session (normally one or two days later) then emphasises a different body part. Using such a split routine, the three or four exercises carried out in session one will emphasise the legs, for example, whilst the following day's session could be for the chest. Split routines effectively allow you to train hard every day, since each trained muscle group is given ample time to recover between training sessions.

The aspect of recovery between strength-training sessions is a vital one. After a training session muscles which have worked hard need time to recover, replenish their energy stores and repair any connective tissue damage that has occurred. It is during the recovery phase between work outs that training adaptations occur, so it is vital that adequate recovery time is taken. Generally it makes good sense to allow at least twenty-four hours between training bouts of the same type or which involve the same muscles in the same way. However, too much time between training sessions is not a good idea, since any adaptations to training only take place if the training stimulus is repeated regularly. Following a single set, or basic multi-set system it is possible to train effectively every other day. Following more demanding multi-set and pyramid systems it makes more sense to split your routine as explained here, performing a series of exercises for the same body part on one day with a series of exercises for another body part being carried out on the next day. Even so, when following a split routine system it still makes sense to take one day of complete recovery each week on which no resistance training is performed at all.

To illustrate the above systems, a number of sample programmes using the different systems discussed are outlined below.

**SINGLE-SET SYSTEM**

Warm up thoroughly. Perform one set of ten repetitions on each of the following exercises. Remember to choose a resistance/weight which only allows you to perform ten reps, with good technique in each case. Allow yourself a rest and recovery period between exercises of ninety seconds.

Squat
Bench press
Leg extension
Shoulder press
Leg curl
Arm curl
Hip extension
Curl-up
Abdominal crunch
Warm down thoroughly

**MULTIPLE-SET SYSTEM**

Warm up thoroughly. Perform four sets of six repetitions on each of the exercises listed in the earlier single-set system example. Allow ninety seconds rest and recovery period between sets and exercises. Warm down thoroughly.

**PYRAMID SYSTEM**

Warm up thoroughly. Using the bench press as an example, choose a weight which allows you to perform the following numbers of repetitions in each set:

| | |
|---|---|
| set 1 : 1 x 15 reps | set 5 : 1 x 6 reps |
| set 2 : 1 x 12 reps | set 6 : 1 x 4 reps |
| set 3 : 1 x 10 reps | set 7 : 1 x 2–3 reps |
| set 4 : 1 x  8 reps | set 8 : 1 x 1–2 reps |

Allow yourself ninety seconds recovery between sets 1–4, with a slightly longer recovery period (three to five minutes) between the more intense sets (5 – 8). If you intend to come down the pyramid, reverse the above, although you may find yourself having to use lighter weights than those used when ascending the pyramid. If not coming down the pyramid finish off the exercise for this body part with one light set of fifteen reps. Warm down thoroughly.

This type of training is very demanding and you should allow yourself two to three days recovery (during which you can train other body parts) before performing this type of session for the same muscles again.

# RESISTANCE TRAINING FOR INCREASED MUSCULAR SIZE

The systems of resistance training outlined in the previous section may be considered as being of value in increasing muscular size, since one of the adaptations to strength training is muscular hypertrophy. However, body-builders have also developed other systems of training which seem to be particularly suited to increasing muscle bulk. Whilst high force development is characteristic of both strength improvement and muscle-building programmes, body-building systems further concentrate on very high volumes of work, limited recovery between sets and more exercises to work muscles throughout every conceivable muscle and joint angle. It is this high force, high volume limited recovery type of work which seems to bring about the greatest change in muscle size and these factors should be borne in mind if significant increases in muscular size are to be observed.

Yet it should be realised that the increases in size exhibited by many body-builders are not often related directly to increases in strength. It would seem that training with muscle hypertrophy in mind does not seem to lead to massive increases in muscular strength. This can be a problem if you are an athlete or sportsperson since your muscle mass may well increase to such an extent which if not mirrored by changes in functional strength, may well lower your effective power-weight ratio. This in turn may decrease your effectiveness as a performer. Training for muscle size often leads to a decrease in the ratio of blood capillaries and mitochondria to muscle cells, as the muscle's increase in size is again not matched by similar massive adaptations in capillary and mitochondrial size and density. Such imbalances would effectively make the body-builder less cardiovascularly and aerobically efficient.

The training considerations for gains in muscle size are well illustrated by considering one system of muscle mass development known as super setting (not to be confused with agonist-antagonist training which is sometimes referred to as super setting by some trainers). In this system at least two and often three exercises for the same body part are chosen. On each exercise, a resistance is used such that only eight to ten repetitions can be performed. The first set of the first exercise is then executed, quickly followed by the first set of the second exercise, followed by the first set of the third exercise. After a short recovery – no more than ninety seconds, the sequence is repeated. It is common to perform three sets of each exercise in this fashion.

Along similar lines are sets of exercises performed to failure, known as exhaustion systems. Here the aim is to repeat an exercise until no more repetitions of that exercise can be performed. This can be done in sets using the same resistance or it can be done using a technique known as stripping. In this system it is common to work up to a resistance (sometimes using a pyramid system) so that only four reps of an exercise can be performed. Having performed four reps, the resistance is lowered by having a helper or helpers remove or strip some of the weight from the training bar or apparatus (using weight stack equipment with a selector pin, this system can just about be performed by an individual on their own). More repetitions should then be performed up until failure, then the weight should be lowered again. Successive decreases in resistance allow several sets to be performed in this fashion. Other exhaustion systems include working to failure on a set and then having your training partner assist you slightly in the exercise so that you can squeeze out three or four more repetitions. This technique is known as forced repping.

These systems of training are thought to be effective in terms of increasing muscular size mainly because of the high volume of high intensity work. This effectively means that all muscle fibres, whatever their characteristics end up having to generate as much force as possible, even when they are fatigued and respond by increasing in cross-sectional area.

Other systems also employed by body-builders to increase muscular size include heavy-negative methods and paused reps. In the heavy-negative system, the exerciser takes advantage of the fact that muscles can handle heavier weights in the negative phase of the movement than in the positive phase. Heavy-negative systems therefore employ the help of a training partner to help you overcome a heavier than normal resistance on the positive phase of the exercise, whilst you are left to control the negative phase on your own. Caution should be employed whilst performing heavy-negative training, since eccentric contractions have been associated with extreme muscle soreness following exercise due to muscle and connective tissue damage.

Paused rep systems can be used within other systems to enable very high forces to be generated at specific joint angles. Furthermore, paused rep training effectively cuts out any advantage to raising and lowering weights which occurs because of the weights' momentum. A typical paused rep sequence would be to take any exercise and perform each repetition in every set, holding one position for two seconds at some phase of the repetition where high forces must be generated. Taking the bench press exercise, the bar could be held for two seconds one inch above the chest before the repetition continues.

Examples of some of the above systems are given in the following programmes.

### SUPER SET SYSTEM

Warm up thoroughly. Choose two or three exercises for the same body part or muscle group or which involve the same muscles in different movements, for example, shoulder press, lateral raise and upright rowing, as in the following circuit:

1 × 10 shoulder press
1 × 10 lateral raise
1 × 10 upright rowing

Move swiftly from one exercise to the next, allowing yourself ninety seconds of rest and recovery between circuits. Perform three circuits. Move on to another muscle group or warm down thoroughly.

### STRIPPING SYSTEM

Warm up thoroughly. Using any exercise such as leg extensions, use a pyramid system to work up to one set of four reps, for example:

set 1 : 1 x 15    set 4 : 1 x 8
set 2 : 1 x 12    set 5 : 1 x 6
set 3 : 1 x 10    set 6 : 1 x 4

Allow yourself ninety seconds recovery between sets.

Having established your weight for the heavy set, recover for five minutes. Then repeat set 6 but this time after four reps, quickly decrease the weight (get the help of a partner beforehand), then perform six to eight reps with this lower weight. Again quickly decrease the weight, performing a set of as many reps as possible. Warm down thoroughly.

# RESISTANCE TRAINING FOR IMPROVED MUSCULAR POWER

Muscular power reflects not only how much force a muscle or muscle group can produce but how quickly that force is generated. Consequently, strength and power do not mean the same and should not be used synonymously; whilst someone may be described as being strong if he or she can lift a very heavy weight, that same person can only be described as being powerful if he or she can lift that heavy weight quickly. Power is effectively a marriage of strength and speed.

In all sports and athletic events, those performers who can develop considerable power, all other things being equal, are almost guaranteed success. Short, explosive sprints on the games field, the throwing of implements, rapid movements on the racquets court, jumping vertically or horizontally – all of these activities require the ability to develop power.

Power training is associated with many of the changes listed for strength training, though the amount of muscular hypertrophy observed as a result of power training may often be less than that seen as a result of pure strength training. This is generally seen as an advantage, since increases in power without dramatic increases in muscle mass lead to a more favourable power–weight ratio. The recruitment of muscle fibres (motor units) and their synchronisation is most marked during power training compared to strength training however, as are cellular changes which make the trained muscles more able to develop high forces very rapidly (it is power training which makes type IIb muscle fibres more like type IIa).

## Assessing Muscular Power

One of the simplest tests of muscular power is the assessment of your 'speed-off-the-mark' over a given distance. All you need to do is measure out a distance, of say thirty metres. Then, having warmed up thoroughly, get a friend to act as your starter and timer and see how quickly you can cover the measured distance. Take the best of three attempts, with a full recovery between each sprint. The test should be standardised as much as possible when it is repeated and you should aim to use the same surface and track for subsequent retests.

Naturally, this test emphasises the explosive power of the locomotor muscles of the lower body. You can look at upper body power by performing medicine ball throws. The following is a good example; lie face up on the floor with your heels touching a strip of marking tape. Hold the medicine ball at arm's length so that it rests on the floor behind your head. From this position try and throw the ball as far as possible past your feet, getting a friend to observe where it first lands. Measure the distance between the ball's landing point and the marker tape. Take the best of three trials.

## Power Training Systems

There are several methods of power training, yet each method relies upon trying to generate high forces at fast speeds. One of the longest established methods works on strength and speed separately. So, a period of pure strength training for appropriate muscle groups is followed by a period of training with slightly lighter weights, where the emphasis is directed to moving the weights at faster speeds. Some coaches have adapted this rather segmented approach and incorporate a speed-training session into a weekly strength-training programme with both programmes using the same exercises. The theory is that the speed which is developed in one session can be carried over to link with the strength being developed in the other sessions as the weeks go by. Certainly this seems to work and as long as speed does not fall and strength improves, or speed increases and strength levels are maintained, power output will be increased. The ratio of speed to strength sessions can obviously be varied according to the time of year and an athlete's or sportsperson's competitive season to make the training most effective. More strength work should be emphasised at the beginning of a winter training period for an athlete with speed sessions taking priority throughout the spring. Obviously, the choice of exercises and activities should reflect the athlete's or sportsperson's competitive activity.

Other methods of speed training can also be harnessed to strength training to make a more complete programme for a performer. If a performer's sport requires him/her to sprint flat out quite frequently over a distance of 20m, it would make sense to improve the strength of the locomotor muscles using a strength programme, whilst at the same time working on sprint speed drills such as are practised by sprinters.

One particular method of power training which is gaining wider acceptance is known as plyometrics. A plyometric exercise is simply one in which a muscle is loaded rapidly as it lengthens, prior to a forceful concentric contraction. One common plyometric activity is depth jumping; standing on a low box, the exerciser jumps down on to the floor. Upon landing, he/she then tries to immediately spring back up into the air, aiming for either vertical height or horizontal distance. Such jumps can be repeated over a series of benches or boxes, with other plyometric exercises including various leaps, bounds, jumps and hops.

Plyometric exercises are thought to enhance explosive power because not only do they develop neuromuscular co-ordination, they also take advantage of a basic physiological reflex response, namely that concentric contractions are much more forceful when they follow eccentric contractions.

Yet plyometric training requires caution and careful execution. As effective as it is, it is best reserved for the very well-conditioned performer since the high loadings placed on muscles and joints can cause injury. Ideally, plyometric training should follow a period (of several months duration) of general strength and introductory power training. A thorough warm up is also essential.

Sample power-training programmes are given below.

### POWER TRAINING

One of the easiest ways to use resistance training to improve power is to structure a performer's programme carefully over a long period. Taking a javelin thrower, for example, the winter is the off season, so for the first few weeks the emphasis can be on general strength work, perhaps using a simple multi-set system. Obviously, skill practices and specific conditioning exercises and training will be performed at the same time. After six to eight weeks of this type of resistance training, pyramid systems of strength training can be introduced in a split-routine programme. As the thrower gets closer to the competitive season, the total volume of general strength training can be reduced, weights lowered and the emphasis placed upon speed in all the training movements and exercises.

### PLYOMETRIC TRAINING

Different types of plyometric programmes can be developed. Remember that the exerciser must possess a high degree of basic foundation strength before attempting any bounding or depth-jumping exercises.

### Plyometric Circuit

Warm up thoroughly. Perform each of the following exercises for thirty seconds, allowing yourself thirty seconds active recovery between sets.

Astride jumps
Two-footed jumps
Hops
Leaps
Burpees

Give yourself five minutes active recovery and repeat the circuit three times. Warm down thoroughly.

# RESISTANCE TRAINING FOR IMPROVED MUSCULAR ENDURANCE

Muscular endurance reflects the ability of a muscle or muscle group to repeatedly exert force and overcome resistance in the absence of fatigue. As with muscular strength, muscular endurance is classified as a health-related component of fitness, since possessing a high degree of muscular endurance is important in carrying out daily tasks without becoming excessively tired. Muscular endurance is also very important with respect to good posture, whether sitting, standing or moving.

It is common to discuss the local muscular endurance (LME) of a muscle or muscle group as well as the general muscular endurance that an individual possesses. Equally, because muscles can generate force whilst either changing or maintaining length both dynamic (eccentric, concentric or isokinetic) and static (isometric) local or general muscular endurance may be discussed.

Changes which are associated with regular local muscular endurance training are perhaps less obvious than those associated with regular size or strength training since many of the changes take place internally without leading to external visible differences. The number and size of blood capillaries in a muscle increase, as do the number and size of the mitochondria. The concentration of enzymes necessary for aerobic energy production also increases. It is these changes which make the muscle more able to repeatedly generate force without becoming fatigued. The amount of contractile protein in the muscle may increase and this in turn may lead to a firmer, harder muscle, but no significant changes in the size of muscles are likely to occur with LME training.

If a general muscular-endurance programme is followed, emphasising all the major muscle groups in the body, then the adaptations mentioned above occur in the exercised muscles. Further, changes occur in the cardio-vascular system generally (as opposed to the specific peripheral changes already mentioned). These can include increases in total blood volume and the concentration of haemoglobin (which carries the oxygen around the body) effectively making the body more efficient at transporting blood to the working muscles. However, general cardio-vascular changes are more noticeable after a programme of aerobic fitness training. (*See* Resistance Training for Improved Aerobic Fitness, pages 42–5.)

# Assessing Muscular Endurance

Just as there are a number of ways of assessing muscular strength, so there are a similar number of ways of assessing muscular endurance. Naturally, it is also possible to try and assess the individual LME of each major muscle group in the body. This is time consuming, however, and it has become common to use one specific, simple field test as an indicator of general muscular endurance. This test is known as a timed sit-up and strictly speaking, is an assessment of the LME (and strength, to a certain extent) of the abdominal muscles.

To perform the test, the person being tested lies flat on the floor with knees bent, feet a comfortable distance apart and arms folded across the chest. The person doing the testing then holds the subject's ankles down so that both feet are kept firmly in contact with the floor at all times. The tester then gives the person being tested the signal to start. The subject then has to curl up off the floor, touch his or her elbows against the thighs (still keeping the arms in contact with the chest) and then curl down to the floor again. The sequence has to be repeated as many times as possible in a thirty-second period. As in all abdominal exercises, it is important to breathe out during the curling-up phase, and breathe in throughout the curling-down movement. Typical scores for this test are given in *Fig 12*.

# Endurance-Training Systems

Once again, there are a number of different endurance-training systems. The common feature that they all have is that they require you to exert less than maximal force repeatedly. Typically, the number of repetitions in one set of an exercise in an endurance

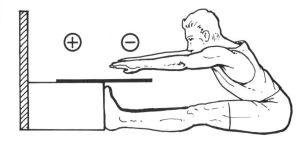

*Fig 12(a)   The timed sit-and-reach test of flexibility.*

| Rating | 20–39 years | 40–59 years |
|---|---|---|
| Poor | less than 17 | less than 12 |
| Fair | 17–19 | 12–15 |
| Average | 20–21 | 16–17 |
| Good | 22–23 | 18–19 |
| Excellent | 24 or more | 20 or more |

*Fig 12(b)   Scoring table for the timed sit-up test.*

programme is fifteen or more. The simplest programmes are single-set systems as described in the strength-training section, with different exercises being chosen for all major muscle groups and performed in sequence. The exercises are usually performed with little (fifteen seconds maximum) recovery between sets/exercises or with no recovery whatsoever. More sets of each exercise may be performed, usually up to three, depending upon the number of repetitions in each set. These sets of each exercise may be performed sequentially, or it is possible to perform one set of one exercise, followed by one set of the next exercise and so on until one complete circuit of exercises has been completed. After a short recovery (say two minutes) additional circuits may then be completed according to fitness. Endurance programmes designed in this fashion are known as circuit systems.

Circuit systems have been shown to be very effective when it comes to improving general muscular endurance and the principles of circuit training can also be used to develop strength and power, although such circuits are less effective than more traditional strength and power programmes such as those given in the appropriate sections of this chapter. Currently two-circuit endurance circuits are very popular. One of these is based on the agonist/antagonist system and requires you to perform one exercise and follow it immediately with an exercise which emphasises the opposite muscle group to the one which was just exercised. This sequence of exercise for one muscle group, followed by exercise for the opposing muscle group is repeated until the whole body has been worked. The other system is known as the peripheral heart action system and aims to get blood moving from one part of the body to another by requiring you to perform one exercise for the upper body, followed by one exercise for the lower body. This sequence is then repeated, until, as before, all the major muscle groups in the body have been exercised. Both systems are effective if executed correctly.

When designing muscular endurance programmes, it should also be considered that there is no reason why specific muscles or parts of the body should not be targeted in one session, as with strength-training and body-building programmes, depending upon the needs and aims of the training individual. It should also be noted that several weeks of general muscular endurance training makes an excellent foundation for more demanding strength or size programmes.

For rapid general or specific muscular endurance gains, train every other day on a general programme or every day on a split routine with one day off each week (as for split routine strength training).

Sample muscular endurance training programmes are given below.

CIRCUIT TRAINING FOR LME
### Example 1 : agonist/antagonist system
Warm up thoroughly. Perform one set of fifteen repetitions on each of the following exercises. Allow yourself thirty seconds active recovery between sets/exercises.

Bench press
Seated row
Seated press behind neck
Pull-ups
Hip extensions
Curl-ups
Leg extension
Leg curl

Repeat the circuit three times, allowing two minutes active recovery between circuits. Warm down thoroughly.

### Example 2 : peripheral heart action circuit
Warm up thoroughly. Perform each exercise for thirty seconds, then perform thirty seconds of traditional aerobic activity (jogging for example) before moving on to the next exercise.

Bench press
Leg press
Shoulder press
Leg extension
Pull-ups
Leg curl
Upright rowing
Heel raise
Abdominal curl

Allow two minutes active recovery between circuits and perform three circuits in total. Warm down thoroughly.

# RESISTANCE TRAINING FOR IMPROVED AEROBIC FITNESS

Aerobic fitness may be considered as being a combination of two components of physical fitness, namely muscular endurance and cardio-respiratory endurance. This is because in order for muscles to work continuously for a prolonged period of time they must be well supplied with nutrients and oxygen. Furthermore, by-products which a muscle may produce as a result of that work (carbon dioxide) need to be excreted from the body if the muscle's work is to be continued effectively. In other words, the ability of a large number of muscles to engage in muscular endurance activities requires a high degree of cardio-respiratory efficiency.

Aerobic fitness training has been linked with many positive health benefits and has been widely researched. Briefly, regular aerobic exercise can reduce your risk of heart and circulatory problems in a number of ways. Certainly, aerobic training improves the efficiency of the heart and lungs and circulation in general (*see* also pages 21–4). The heart for example becomes a better pump with regular aerobic exercise and its stroke volume increases (the left ventricle fills more and also grows larger in internal diameter with progressive training). As a result, one of the most obvious reflections of improved aerobic fitness is a lowering of an individual's heart rate, both at rest and during physical activity, since cardiac output can be maintained with fewer beats as a greater volume of blood is being sent around the body with each beat (cardiac output = stroke volume x heart rate). Note that this is in contrast to the effect that strength training has on the heart. Progressive strength (and power) training may lead to an increase in the thickness of the left ventricular wall, allowing the heart to eject blood more forcefully, but there is invariably no change in the internal diameter of the ventricle itself. Regular aerobic exercise also leads to improved blood flow to the heart. Aerobic exercise has been shown to help lower blood pressure, as well as altering the level of dangerous circulating fats in the bloodstream. It is changes such as these and others, which have made aerobic exercise such a useful tool in lowering the risk of heart attacks in the population in general.

Other physiological changes associated with aerobic fitness training include those which have already been mentioned in the previous section dealing with the development of muscular endurance. Additionally, it is worth noting that regular, continuous, long duration (twenty minutes plus) aerobic exercise is very useful when it comes to changing one's body composition, since it is precisely this type of low intensity, long duration, aerobic physical activity which uses significant amounts of stored body fat as fuel for muscular work.

# Assessing Aerobic Fitness

Whilst there are numerous tests for aerobic fitness, one of the simplest field tests which can be performed is known as the one-and-a-half mile run and was developed by Dr. Kenneth Cooper. Like all running tests, it suffers from the fact that running technique, pace judgement, weather conditions and the running surface itself will all influence the final result and hence the final score (or rating) that is achieved. Yet, if the test is repeated under the same conditions it is a reliable indicator of the improvement in aerobic fitness associated with the training programme being pursued.

To carry out the test you need an accurately measured distance of one-and-a-half miles. An athletics track is ideal for this (on a standard track you will need to complete six laps). Having sorted out your course, warm up thoroughly and attempt to cover the distance as quickly as possible through a combination of jogging/running. The best times are normally associated with running at a steady pace, speeding up towards the end if this feels possible. Make a note of the time it takes you to complete the distance, warm down thoroughly and then compare your time with those in *Fig 13* (supplied by the National Coaching Foundation).

# Aerobic Fitness Training Systems

For an exercise to be considered aerobic it needs to involve large muscle groups in regular, rhythmical contractions. As a rough

| Age (years) | very poor | poor | fair | good | very good | excellent | superb |
|---|---|---|---|---|---|---|---|
| **Men** | | | | | | | |
| 17–29 | 16.30+ | 14.30+ | 12.00+ | 10.15+ | 8.15+ | 7.30+ | 6.45+ |
| 30–34 | 17.00+ | 15.00+ | 12.30+ | 10.30+ | 8.30+ | 7.45+ | 7.00+ |
| 35–39 | 17.30+ | 15.30+ | 13.00+ | 10.45+ | 8.45+ | 8.00+ | 7.15+ |
| 40–44 | 18.00+ | 16.00+ | 13.30+ | 11.00+ | 9.00+ | 8.15+ | 7.30+ |
| 45–49 | 18.30+ | 16.30+ | 14.00+ | 11.15+ | 9.15+ | 8.30+ | 7.45+ |
| over 50 | 19.00+ | 17.00+ | 14.30+ | 11.30+ | 9.30+ | 8.45+ | 8.00+ |
| **Women** | | | | | | | |
| 17–29 | 19.48+ | 17.24+ | 14.24+ | 12.18+ | 9.54+ | 9.00+ | 8.06+ |
| 30–34 | 20.24+ | 18.00+ | 15.00+ | 12.36+ | 10.12+ | 9.18+ | 8.24+ |
| 35–39 | 21.00+ | 18.36+ | 15.36+ | 12.54+ | 10.30+ | 9.36+ | 8.42+ |
| 40–44 | 21.36+ | 19.12+ | 16.12+ | 13.12+ | 10.48+ | 9.54+ | 9.00+ |
| 45–49 | 22.12+ | 19.48+ | 16.48+ | 13.30+ | 11.06+ | 10.30+ | 9.36+ |
| over 50 | 22.48+ | 20.24+ | 17.24+ | 13.48+ | 11.24+ | 10.30+ | 9.36+ |

*Fig 13   Scoring table for the Cooper one-and-a-half mile run.*

guide, it should also be of moderate intensity, so that it can be performed continuously for upwards of ten minutes. Heart rate methods of monitoring exercise intensity have been developed, yet for reasons explained earlier these are not very suitable during resistance training. As a guide, moderate intensity, aerobic activity should allow you to just about hold a conversation as you exercise. Traditional aerobic activities include brisk walking, jogging, running, cycling and swimming.

There is really only one system of resistance training that is suitable for improving aerobic fitness and that is circuit training. The aim should be to complete around fifteen to twenty repetitions of an exercise before moving on to the next exercise in the sequence (as outlined earlier in the previous section on endurance training). Alternatively, aim to perform as many repetitions of one exercise – in say thirty seconds – as possible, before moving on to the next exercise in the circuit. However, it is possible to get greater aerobic fitness improvement if instead of moving on to the next exercise in the sequence, you perform a typical aerobic exercise activity for at least thirty seconds. This could be jogging, cycling or rowing – all of which can be performed easily in the gymnasium setting.

Taking this idea one step further there is no reason why the aerobic activity phase between sets should not be lengthened (try two minutes) time permitting, so that more traditional aerobic activity is performed during the circuit. Another alternative is to have short aerobic activity bouts between sets (thirty to sixty seconds), with longer (five minutes) aerobic activity bouts between circuits. Obviously, the more time that is spent performing the aerobic activity, the greater the aerobic training effect. With such a design, try and balance the aerobic work with the specific LME work according to needs and training aims.

**AEROBIC CIRCUIT**

This following circuit is known affectionately as a sweat circuit. Warm up thoroughly, jog or cycle for five minutes. Perform the following exercises for sixty seconds, and jog or cycle for two minutes between exercises.

Bench press
Squat
Single arm rowing (thirty seconds each arm)
Leg extension
Shoulder press
Leg curl
Hip extensions
Curl-up

After each circuit, jog or cycle for five minutes. Perform three circuits. Warm down thoroughly.

# RESISTANCE TRAINING TO SHAPE YOUR BODY

One of the growth areas in fitness training has been that of body shaping or body sculpting. As the terms imply, the aim of such exercise systems is to improve the shape of your body through resistance training.

The benefits and physiological adaptations associated with body shaping will largely depend upon the type of training employed during the body shaping programme. It is common to use a number of different training systems for different components of fitness to achieve an individual's desired aim. However, once an improvement in body shape has been achieved, it has been observed that the improvement in shape and physical appearance often leads to an improvement in how the individual sees him/herself. In other words, the improvement in shape leads to a more positive self image. As a consequence, the trained, fitter, more shapely individual often becomes more confident and assertive.

# Assessing Shape

The easiest way to assess your shape is by measuring the girths of various parts of the body. Common girth measurements include bicep (upper arm), chest/bust, waist, hips, thigh and calf. In addition, it is also useful to measure your height and weight. Girths should always be taken using a tape measure which does not stretch (in the lab, a steel tape is preferred) and all girth measurements need to be repeated at exactly the same site if possible. When weighing yourself, bear in mind that different scales will give slightly different values according to how they have been calibrated. Always try therefore to weigh yourself using the same scales.

A full-length mirror is also of value in assessing your shape and how it changes as a result of regular training, but you must be honest with yourself! Another useful measure is to assess your body composition, which can indicate how much fat you are carrying. To do this accurately is difficult, but a simple procedure has been developed by the physiologist, Jack Wilmore. This assessment relies upon the fact that in most men excess fat accumulates around the waist, whilst in most women fat accumulates around the hips. The test requires only two measurements. Men need to measure their weight (in pounds) and their waist (in inches) at navel level. Women need to measure their height (in inches, no shoes) and take their hip measurements (also in inches) at the maximum protrusion of their buttocks. Having taken the necessary measurements then compare these measurements to the *Fig 14* overleaf. In each case, place a straight edge (a ruler for example) so that it runs from body-weight to waist girth (men) or from hip girth to height (women). Read off your estimated per cent body fat at the point where the ruler crosses the middle line.

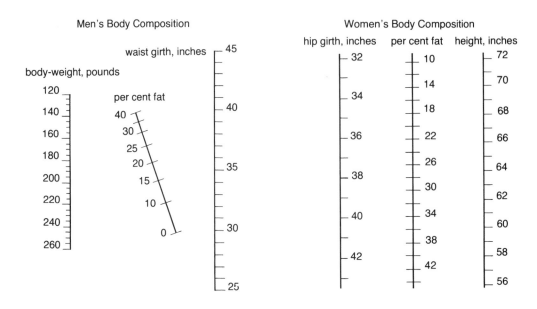

*Fig 14  Estimation of body composition.*

# Body-Shaping Systems

There are no specific body-shaping systems as such, rather, body shaping tends to combine many of the systems already described. For example, if your body shaping aim is to increase the size of your muscles, then you should refer directly to the appropriate section of this book (pages 35–7) and follow any of the programme designs and systems outlined there. If your specific aim is to increase the definition of your limbs, to make them appear longer perhaps, you may then like to perform a programme of body-building for several weeks, followed by a programme of endurance or aerobic fitness work. The building programme can be kept quite separate from the endurance/aerobic programme or it can be performed in tandem by changing the emphasis. For example, several weeks of training could be structured so that three training sessions each week are devoted to increasing muscular size, with one session per week emphasising aerobic fitness. After this phase of training one of the size sessions could be swapped for an endurance session and the training programme could proceed in this fashion for several more weeks and so on. Training like this is very varied and hence interesting and means that a wide variety of fitness and shape benefits are developed as the training progresses. Furthermore, because there is always some work being performed for each training aim or fitness component, specific fitness adaptations, having been achieved, are largely maintained. This type of training is also often referred to as cross-training.

Body-shaping programmes can also include specific work for specific muscle groups, if necessary, with more work being performed on the legs, for example, if these are a problem area. However, it should be pointed out here that if you are carrying excess fat in a region, doing extra work for the muscles under that fat area will not move the fat. This is because fat used as fuel for exercise comes from all over the body and not from the specific site being exercised. To move fat from any part of the body requires the emphasis to be placed on aerobic exercise of long duration. At the same time, an individual's diet should be analysed and modified to make it more appropriate for fat loss.

# RESISTANCE TRAINING FOR IMPROVED SPORTS PERFORMANCE

The benefits of regular resistance training for sports performers were pointed out in the Introduction. Having read the preceding sections of this chapter, the advantages than can be gained by the sportsman or woman through this type of training should be more than obvious.

Yet when designing sports-specific programmes, the individual (or coach) should ensure that the resistance-training programme is as appropriate as possible for the individual and takes into account both the strengths and weaknesses of the performer and the demands of his or her sport. (These points have been made elsewhere in the text, yet they are important enough to merit being repeated.)

Addressing these issues requires a careful analysis of the performer to find his/her fitness weaknesses (as indicated in each section of this chapter) and then working on them in a way which allows the fitness components which are developed, to be as relevant as possible to the sports technique itself. For example, if a performer lacks aerobic fitness, yet his/her sport does not require a high degree of this aspect of fitness, is there any great need to emphasise aerobic work in training? Obviously, this does not make sense, neither does emphasising the development of force at slow speeds when an individual's sport requires rapid force development. This is not to say that general training has no value, rather the specific nature of fitness and sport must always be considered in the design of effective sports-conditioning programmes.

It is also important not to neglect the skill aspects of a person's sport. Much can be achieved in the gym, but specific skills and practices should not be pushed to one side in favour of more gym work.

Generally, having identified the shortcomings of the individual performer and the demands of their sport, it makes most sense to work on fitness and skill by breaking the performer's year into training phases or periods. This organisation of training aims is known as periodisation. Different emphases can then be placed on fitness components and skill drills according to the time of year and a steady, relevant progression in both specific fitness and skill will be achieved.

# 4 Warming Up and Warming Down for Resistance Training

Every well-structured exercise or training session should include a warming-up phase, during which the body is prepared for subsequent and more strenuous physical activity and a warming-down period, during which the body is brought back to normal following the training phase itself.

The warm-up phase should have two major aims in mind. Firstly, there should be an attempt to increase the temperature of the body. This is because a warm body is less likely to be injured, since muscles and connective tissues become more 'elastic' in general. Furthermore, when the body is warm, nerve impulses travel more readily and it is easier for the various processes involved in energy production to take place. Secondly, a good warm up should include exercises which take the limbs, muscles and joints through their current range of movement gradually and progressively.

To achieve this it makes sense to dress warmly in several layers of clothing, particularly during cold weather and when exercising outdoors. Then you should involve the body in some large muscle group activity which emphasises regular and rhythmical contractions – jogging or any basic aerobic activity. The intensity of the exercise activity chosen should be light and should only promote the onset of light sweating at the most. The time taken for this to occur will vary according to the environmental conditions and the individual, yet five to ten minutes should suffice. Following this whole body activity, the exerciser should then perform some easy, rhythmical exercises (such as those given here), before carrying out some light stretching for the major muscle groups and joints that will be involved in the exercise phase which is to follow. Each stretch employed in this phase need only be held for approximately six seconds and this phase of pre-activity stretching is often referred to as preparatory stretching.

If your training is going to be particularly demanding it makes sense to spend more time warming up and to include some specific exercises. If you are going to emphasise leg work and your session includes heavy squatting, prepare your body for this by carrying out a few sets (involving high repetitions) of light squats either before or after your preparatory stretching. Also, if you do not fancy performing any form of traditional whole-body aerobic exercise for the first part of your warm up, an alternative is to put together a general endurance or aerobic circuit and to do this using very light resistances instead, before moving on to your training phase.

Following your training phase, you should allow your body to return to normal by performing some low intensity, whole-body movements as before. This time however, gradually decrease the intensity of the exercise activity until your heart rate and breathing pattern are nearer normal. Then, keep warm by replacing any clothing you may have discarded whilst you were training and perform another stretching sequence. This time, hold each stretch for up to thirty seconds, easing further into the stretch exercise if the sensation of stretch subsides – this is known as developmental stretching. Remember that for a stretch exercise to be effective you should gradually ease into the stretch as far as possible and then hold that position. You should never bounce or force yourself into any position since this invariably leads to injury. Stretching following strenuous exercise is very useful since it not only increases your range of movement and hence your flexibility, but it also seems to help prevent muscle soreness associated with vigorous (or unaccustomed) physical activity.

A few simple, warming-up exercises are included in this chapter, along with some simple stretches. Read the instructions accompanying each exercise very carefully. Use these, or similar exercises in the design of your warming-up and warming-down phases.

# WARMING-UP EXERCISES

There are numerous exercises which can be used as part of your warm-up phase. The following few exercises, coupled with some whole-body activity are a few examples. Whichever exercises you employ in this phase of your exercise session, however, make sure that you perform them in a smooth and controlled fashion.

## Posture (*Fig 15*)

Prior to exercise, it is always a good idea to check your posture. Your feet should be a comfortable distance apart (approximately shoulder-width) and your weight should be evenly balanced. Your pelvis should feel centred – in other words your abdomen should be pulled in and your buttocks need to be tucked under. Your spine should be

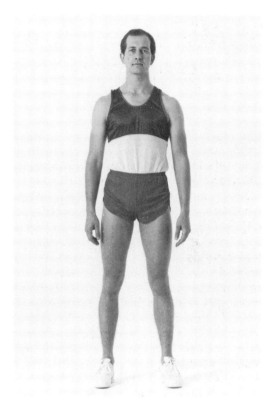

*Fig 15   Posture.*

long, your shoulders down away from your ears and your arms loosely by your sides. You should feel tall, yet relaxed. Try and emphasise these postural pointers throughout your exercise programme as appropriate.

## Shoulder Circles (*Fig 16*)

Stand tall with good posture. Raise your right shoulder up towards your ear, take it backwards then down again in a circular motion. Repeat twelve times with a steady rhythm. Repeat the sequence with the other shoulder.

Having performed the exercise with each shoulder, circle both shoulders at the same time twelve times. Breathe comfortably throughout both exercises.

49

Fig 16    Shoulder circles.

Fig 17 Arm circles.

# Arm Circles (*Fig 17*)

Stand tall with good posture. Raise one arm forward, lift it up and take it back in a continuous circling motion. Keep your spine long throughout. Repeat twelve times with each arm.

Having performed the exercise with each arm, repeat the sequence twelve times. Repeat for another twelve, this time with both arms together, avoiding the tendency to arch the spine. Breathe comfortably throughout both exercises.

# Side Bends (*Fig 18*)

Stand tall with good posture, feet slightly wider than hip-width, hands on hips. Keep your spine long and lift up and over to one side, return to centre, then lift up and over to the other side. Avoid the tendency to lean forwards or backwards. Repeat twelve times on each side with a steady rhythm, breathing

Fig 18    Side bends.

50

out as you bend to the side and in as you return.

## Waist Twists (*Fig 19*)

Stand tall with good posture. Take your feet a little wider apart, bend your knees slightly and rest your hands on your hips. Keeping your spine long, try and turn your shoulders round to the side, whilst still keeping your hips facing forwards. Go as far round to the side as you can and hold your furthermost position before coming back to the centre. Repeat sixteen times on each side, breathing comfortably throughout the exercise sequence.

## Half Squats (*Figs 20 and 21*)

Stand tall with good posture. Place your hands out in front of you for balance, then bend your knees so that your thighs end up parallel to the floor. Hold this position momentarily then under control return to your starting position, straightening your legs fully before continuing. Repeat the exercise following a steady rhythm twenty-four times.

Keep your spine long throughout and ensure that your knees are always pointing in the same direction as your toes. Breathe in as you descend and out as you rise.

*Fig 19   Waist twists.*

*Figs 20 & 21   Half squats.*

# STRETCHING EXERCISES

Ease into each of the following stretch positions as far as possible, whilst still feeling comfortable. As part of the warm-up phase, hold each stretch for six seconds, before moving on to the next exercise. As part of the warm-down phase, hold each stretch for thirty seconds, easing further forward into the stretch position as the sensation of stretch subsides.

## Chest Stretch (*Fig 22*)

Stand tall with good posture. Place your hands, loosely clasped, on the small of your back. Keeping your spine long and your shoulders down, try and bring your elbows together, holding your furthermost position. You will feel the stretch in your chest. Breathe easily throughout the exercise.

## Upper Back Stretch (*Fig 23*)

Stand tall with good posture. Bend your knees slightly and tilt your pelvis under as illustrated. Now interlock your fingers, pushing your hands away from your chest, rounding your upper back and tilting your head to look downwards.

You will feel the stretch between your shoulder blades and lower down your back. Breathe easily throughout the exercise.

## Spine and Trunk Twist (*Fig 24*)

Sit upright on the floor with your legs out in front of you. Bend your right leg up towards you, placing the right foot on the outside of your left knee. Keeping your spine long and your shoulders down away from your ears, twist round so that your shoulders face

*Fig 22   Chest stretch.*

*Fig 23   Upper back stretch.*

*Fig 24   Spine and trunk twist.*

*Fig 25   Seated groin stretch.*

to the side. Use your left arm as a lever to ease as far round as possible and use your right arm for balance.

You will feel the stretch throughout the trunk and spine. Repeat on both sides, breathing easily throughout the exercise.

## Seated Groin Stretch
## (*Fig 25*)

Sit tall on the floor with good posture. Bend your legs up towards you, placing the soles of your feet together and allow your knees to fall towards the floor. Keep your spine long and your shoulders down away from your ears and rest your hands on your calves or ankles. If you find it difficult to sit upright in this position, use your hands behind you for balance. You will feel the stretch along the insides of your thighs and groin.

To increase the stretch and to stretch the hamstrings at the same time, maintain your long spine position whilst hinging forward from your hips as far as possible, holding your furthermost position.

Having done this, relax your back, moving towards the floor. You will now feel more stretch in the buttocks and hamstrings. Again, hold your furthermost position. Breathe easily throughout all of these movements.

## Standing Calf Stretch
## (*Figs 26 and 27*)

Stand tall with one leg in front of the other facing a wall or support. Lean forward, placing your hands against the wall at shoulder-height. Keep your hips facing forward. Ease your back leg out as far behind you as possible whilst still keeping the heel pressed firmly into the floor. Your spine should be long. You will feel the stretch in the calf of the back leg. Repeat with both legs. To stretch the calf lower down, adopt the same position, but bend the back knee slightly (*see Fig 26*),

*Figs 26 & 27   Standing calf stretch.*

still keeping the heel down. Repeat on both sides. Breathe easily throughout all these movements.

## Standing Quadriceps Stretch (*Fig 28*)

Stand tall with good posture. Holding on to a support, reach behind you with your left arm to loosely grasp your left foot. Ease your foot towards your buttocks whilst keeping your spine long and your bottom tucked under. You will feel the stretch in the front of the left thigh. Repeat on both sides, breathing easily throughout.

## Standing Hamstring Stretch (*Fig 29*)

Stand tall with good posture. Bend at the knees and hips until you can easily rest your chest on your thighs. Reach round with your arms and grasp behind your legs, holding your chest and thighs closely together. From this position, gently try and straighten your legs, whilst still keeping your chest firmly pressed against your thighs. You will feel the stretch along the backs of your legs. Breathe easily throughout this exercise.

*Fig 29    Standing hamstring stretch.*

*Fig 28    Standing quadriceps stretch.*

*Fig 30  Lying hip and thigh stretch.*

## Lying Hip and Thigh Stretch (*Fig 30*)

Lie flat on your back with your lower back pressed into the floor. Bring your right knee up to your chest, holding it there with loosely clasped hands. Keep your other leg firmly stretched out along the floor with your foot flexed. You will feel the stretch along the front of the thigh and around the hips and buttocks. Hold the stretch for six seconds and repeat on the other side, breathing easily throughout.

# 5 Resistance-Training Exercises

There are many hundreds of different resistance-training exercises. Commonly, these can be looked at in two main groups: exercises involving one's own body-weight and exercises involving some other form of resistance, whether that of an object, partner, or weight-training equipment in general.

Some of the most common exercises in both groups are represented in this chapter. They can be used, along with any others, to structure any of the training programmes outlined earlier in this book. The equipment needed for the second group of exercises emphasise the most commonly available resistance-training apparatus, namely barbells, dumb-bells and a multi-gym. This does not infer that this type of equipment is superior to any of the cam, or hydraulic-type systems of resistance-training equipment. Such apparatus can obviously be used, in accordance with the manufacturer's instructions, to structure any of the resistance-training programmes mentioned in the text. Each brand of equipment will have its own specific rules regarding the positioning of the body and how the resistance is varied. However, if you are familiar with the exercises given here, working out which machines are for which muscles and how you should position yourself on the equipment in order to perform the exercise is an extremely simple task.

As with all of the exercises included in this book, read the instructions carefully and thoroughly before attempting them. You should also bear the following safety rules in mind when using resistance-training apparatus:

Warm up thoroughly
Exercise from a firm and stable base
Wear suitable shoes
Lift and lower weights with a straight back, bending at the knees
Only add or remove weights from a bar when it is safely on the floor
Always check any equipment that you are about to use for safety, including the tightness of any collars
Get the help of a partner for awkward free-weight (barbell or dumb-bell) exercises
Adjust any equipment used according to the manufacturer's recommendations
Maintain control of any weights you are using at all times, performing each exercise smoothly, without jerking
Warm down thoroughly

Finally, do not train if you feel at all unwell or ill, or if you have just eaten a heavy meal.

# BODY-WEIGHT EXERCISES

## Press-Ups (*Figs 31 and 32*)

For the muscles of the chest, front of shoulder and back of upper arm.

Assume the basic starting position as illustrated. Note that the hands are underneath the shoulders and that there is a straight line from the ankles through the knees, hips and shoulders. From this position, bend your arms so that your chest moves closer to the floor. Go as far as you can, hold your position for a moment, then straighten your arms and repeat. As you get fitter, you should aim to get to a position where your chest touches the floor. Breathe in as you lower yourself to the floor, and out on the return movement.

The exercise can be made easier by modifying the starting position and beginning the movement from your knees and it can be made progressively harder by starting with your feet on a bench. (The same technical rules apply.)

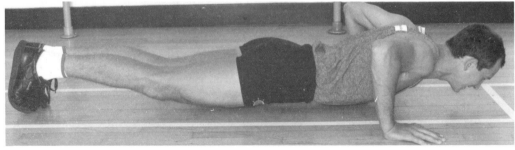

*Figs 31 & 32  Press-ups.*

# Bench (Chair) Dips
## (*Figs 33 and 34*)

For the muscles at the back of the upper arm, front of shoulder and chest.

Using a bench or chair for support, assume the starting position as illustrated. Now lower your bottom to the floor by bending your elbows. Just before your bottom touches the floor, hold the position, then fully straighten your arms to return to your starting position and repeat. Breathe in as you lower and out on the return movement.

The exercise can be made easier by having the knees bent.

*Figs 33 & 34   Bench dips.*

# Pull-Ups (*Figs 35 and 36*)

For the muscles of the upper back and front of upper arm.

A pull-up bar, pull-up frame or gymnasium beam can be used for this exercise. Grasp the bar firmly with either an overgrasp or under-grasp (an overgrasp involves the back muscles more) and hang at full arm's length (you may have to bend your legs to do this). From this long hanging position, pull yourself up so that your head comes up past the bar. Hold this uppermost position for a moment, then under control return to your starting position and repeat. Breathe in as you rise and out on the return movement.

The exercise can be made progressively more demanding by adding weights to the ankles.

*Figs 35 & 36   Pull-ups.*

# Hip Extensions
## (*Figs 37 and 38*)

For the muscles of the lower back and spine, buttocks and hamstrings.

Lie face down on a box or high bench, loosely grasping its sides, so that your legs are hanging off the edge as illustrated. Keeping your legs straight and together, raise them up so that they are parallel to the floor. Hold this position momentarily, then slowly lower your legs towards the floor and repeat. Breathe in as you raise your legs and out as you lower them.

This exercise can be made progressively more difficult by adding weights to your ankles (do this cautiously).

*Figs 37 & 38   Hip extensions.*

# Curl-Ups (*Figs 39 and 40*)

For the muscles at the front of the trunk.

Lie flat on the floor, knees bent at an angle of approximately ninety degrees. Rest your fingertips loosely on the side of your head, keeping your elbows back. Making sure that your lower back is pressed into the floor at all times, smoothly curl your head and shoulders up off the floor. Look upwards and ahead. The fitter you are, the higher off the floor you should curl. Having reached your uppermost position, curl down slowly. As your shoulders touch the floor again, repeat the sequence. Breathe out as you curl-up and in as you curl-down.

If you curl-up, twisting round to the side as you curl, you will work the side abdominals more. Remember to work both sides equally by twisting first to one side then the other.

Both these exercises can be made more demanding by working on an incline board. Bear in mind however, that the held-down position of your feet allows the hip flexor muscles to do more of the work. On an incline board do make a conscious effort consequently to curl-up and avoid the temptation to come up or down with a flat back. Do not jerk through any part of the movement.

*Figs 39 & 40   Curl-ups.*

## Abdominal Crunches (*Figs 41 and 42*)

For the muscles at the front of the trunk.

Lie flat on the floor, with your lower legs resting on a bench or chair so that your hips are directly under your knees. Rest your fingertips loosely by the side of your head or loosely clasp your hands behind your head.

From this position curl-up as in the previous exercise so that your elbows touch your knees. Hold this position momentarily, then curl-down under control. As your shoulders touch the floor, repeat. Breathe out as you curl-up and in on the return.

As with the previous exercise, twisting to either side as you crunch works the side abdominal muscles more.

*Figs 41 & 42    Abdominal crunches.*

# Reverse Curls
## (*Figs 43 and 44*)

For the muscles at the front of the trunk.

Lie flat on the floor with your arms by your sides, legs raised so that they are slightly bent at the knee and directly above your hips. From this position, breathe out and try and raise your hips a couple of inches off the floor, aiming to press your heels up towards the ceiling. Hold your uppermost position momentarily, before lowering your hips, breathing in as you do so. Repeat.

*Figs 43 & 44   Reverse curls.*

## 'U' Sits (*Figs 45 and 46*)

For the muscles at the front of the trunk.

This exercise is basically a combination of the basic curl and the reverse curl. Start from the reverse curl position, but have your arms raised so that they are directly above your shoulders. From this position, try and raise your shoulders and hips off the floor at the same time, breathing out as you do so. Hold your uppermost position momentarily, before returning to your starting position, breathing in as you do so. Repeat.

Naturally there are many more exercises which just involve one's own body-weight which can be performed. This is particularly so if you have access to a traditional gymnasium which features wall bars, climbing frames, ropes, boxes and benches.

The obvious progression from using just your own body-weight is to start using resistance supplied by a partner or by using simple apparatus such as medicine balls. A partner for example, can sit upon your shoulders so that heel raises and squats can be made more demanding, whilst medicine balls can be used with great effect to exercise and condition the muscles of the upper body and trunk which are primarily involved in throwing and pushing actions. Many medicine ball exercises are used by athletes such as discus and javelin throwers and shot putters. Coaching manuals written for these events include many variations and illustrations of these.

The following group of exercises emphasise what are commonly called the locomotor

*Figs 45 & 46   'U' sits.*

*Fig 46*

muscles of the body. These muscles are those which are responsible for travelling either vertically or horizontally and mainly include the muscles of the lower body and trunk.

## Astride Bench Jumps (*Figs 47 and 48*)

Stand with your feet either side of a low bench. Now jump up to place your feet together on the bench and quickly jump down to your starting position again and repeat, breathing easily throughout.

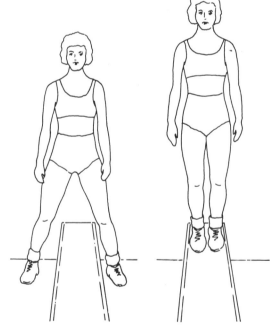

*Figs 47 & 48   Astride bench jumps.*

# Bench Leaps (*Fig 49*)

Stand at the end of a long bench with your feet together. Keeping your feet together, carry out small two-footed jumps, criss-crossing the length of the bench. Turn round at the end of the bench and repeat in the other direction. Breathe easily throughout the exercise.

# Squat Thrusts (Single Leg) (*Figs 50 and 51*)

Assume a basic press-up position as illustrated (note that the hands are under the shoulders and the spine is long). Now bring one knee towards the chest to touch the floor underneath you, taking some of your bodyweight, then smoothly bring the opposite leg underneath you, whilst forcefully extending the bent leg. Breathe easily throughout.

*Fig 49   Bench leaps.*

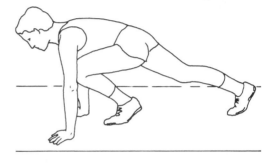

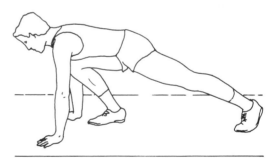

*Figs 50 & 51   Squat thrusts (single leg).*

67

## Squat Thrusts (Both Legs) (*Figs 52 and 53*)

Modify the previous exercise by bringing both legs up to the chest in one movement, then shooting them both out together. Make sure that you go through as full a range of movement as possible. Breathe easily throughout.

## Burpees (*Figs 54–6*)

A burpee is basically an extension of the squat thrust (both legs).

It differs from the squat thrust in that having brought the knees up under the chest, you then forcefully straighten your legs to jump up off the floor, extending the body at the

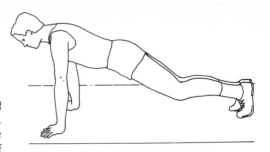

Figs 52 & 53   Squat thrusts (both legs).

Figs 54–6   Burpees.

68

same time. As you land you bend at the knees and hips, place the hands on the floor to take your body-weight and then shoot your legs out behind you.

## Two-Footed Jumps (*Fig 57*)

Stand tall with both feet together. From this position jump forward aiming to cover as much distance as possible. Upon landing, repeat as quickly as possible. Aim to cover the same distance with each jump. Breathe easily throughout.

## Hops (*Fig 58*)

Starting with either leg, hop – aiming for distance as well as height. Start with little hops to begin with, then progress to large hopping movements, kicking out one leg behind you to add extra impetus to the movement. Carry out the same number of hops with both legs.

*Fig 58   Hops.*

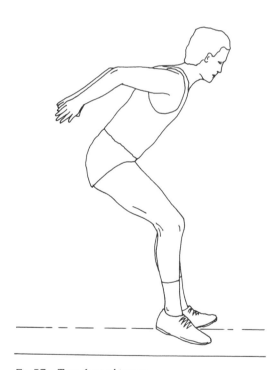

*Fig 57   Two-footed jumps.*

## Obstacle Leaps (*Fig 59*)

Boxes, benches and chairs can be arranged in a sequence to form an obstacle course. Make sure that the obstacle heights are well within your capabilities. In this example, a light chair has been used. Jump off with two feet clearing each obstacle.

If a chair is used, make sure you jump so that if your feet do strike it, the chair will fall with you.

## Leaps (*Fig 60*)

A leap is like a large step in the air. To practise the technique, take large running steps to begin with. Then modify these so that you are aiming for height. As your leading foot lands, leap off it and change legs as you fly through the air, alternating your legs as you cover distance. Aim to cover the same amount of ground with each leap.

*Fig 59   Obstacle leaps.*

*Fig 60     Leaps.*

## Depth Jumps (*Figs 61–3*)

There are many types of depth jumps. It is common however, to jump off a low box, on to the floor. As soon as you land, you should be thinking of springing up, either for vertical distance, horizontal distance, or to land on another box or bench, before proceeding immediately with the next bound or jump in the sequence.

## EXERCISES USING BARBELLS AND DUMB-BELLS

The following series of exercises involves the use of simple barbell and dumb-bell equip-ment, although occasionally a bench or pair of squat stands are also necessary. If purchas-ing such items of equipment, remember that it is better to buy a variety of smaller weight discs than a few large ones, since these will give you the option of putting together bar-bells and dumb-bells of many different weights, so allowing you to perform a greater variety of exercises.

## Bench Press (*Figs 64 and 65*)

For the muscles of the chest, front of shoul-der and back of upper arm.

Lie with your back flat on a bench, making sure that your lower back is firmly pressed into the support. Hold a barbell at arm's

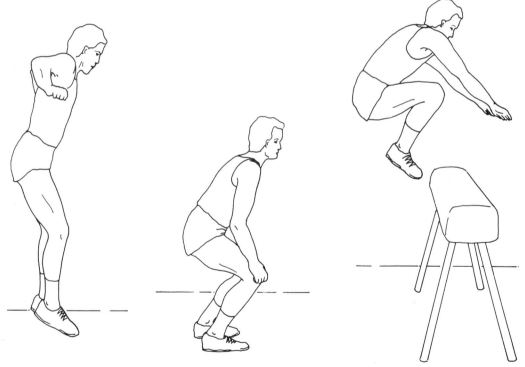

*Figs 61–3   Depth jumps.*

length with a wide grip above your chest (you will need the help of a partner and/or stands for this). Steadily lower the bar so that it touches the middle of your chest, then press it upwards to arm's length again. Do *not* lock out your arms. Repeat the sequence.

Make sure that your elbows are under the bar at all times and that your grip is firm, with the weight of the bar comfortably over the heel of the palm. Breathe in as you lower the bar and out as you raise it.

*Figs 64 & 65   Bench press.*

# Arm (Bicep) Curl
## (*Figs 66 and 67*)

For the muscles at the front of the upper arm.

Stand tall with your feet hip- or shoulder-width apart. Grip a barbell (undergrasp) with your hands shoulder-width apart. Maintain your upright position with your arms close to your sides and smoothly bend at the elbows to raise the bar towards the chest. Return the bar under control to the starting position and repeat. Make sure that you work through as full a range of movement as possible and avoid the tendency to lean forwards or backwards when lifting or lowering the bar.

Breathe in as you raise the bar and out as you lower it.

*Figs 66 & 67   Arm curl with barbell.*

## Alternate Dumb-Bell Curl (*Figs 68 and 69*)

For the muscles at the front of the upper arm.

Stand tall, with your feet hip- or shoulder-width apart, grasping a dumb-bell in each hand. Keeping your upper arms close to your body at all times, bend one arm at the elbow, raising the dumb-bell to the shoulder, twisting the weight through ninety degrees as you do so. Return the dumb-bell under control to the starting position and repeat with the other arm.

Breathe in as you raise the weights and out as you return to the starting position.

*Figs 68 & 69   Alternate dumb-bell curl.*

# Single-Arm Rowing
## (*Figs 70 and 71*)

For the muscles of the upper back and those at the front of the upper arm.

Assume the position as illustrated. Note that your back should be parallel with the floor and that the dumb-bell is directly below your shoulder. Smoothly bring the dumb-bell to your chest, hold the uppermost position, then return the weight to arm's length. Repeat on both sides.

Breathe in as you raise the dumb-bell to the chest and out on the return movement.

*Figs 70 & 71   Single-arm rowing.*

# Side (Lateral) Raise
## (*Figs 72 and 73*)

For the muscles of the shoulders and upper back.

Stand tall with your feet approximately hip-width apart, holding a dumb-bell in each hand. Your arms should be slightly bent at the elbows. From this position, raise the dumb-bells out to the side so that they are approximately in line with your head. Hold this position for a moment, then lower the weights under control to the starting position and repeat. Avoid the tendency to throw the dumb-bells upwards and do not lean forwards or backwards as you do this exercise.

Breathe in as you raise your arms and out as you lower them.

# Seated Press Behind Neck
## (*Figs 74 and 75*)

For the muscles of the shoulders, upper back and backs of the upper arms.

Sit tall on a stable bench with a bar resting comfortably across your shoulders/upper back, holding it there with a wide grip. Smoothly press the barbell upwards to arm's length, yet do not lock out your elbows. Return the barbell under control until it just touches the back of your neck and repeat the sequence.

Breathe in as you press the bar upwards and out on the return movement.

*Figs 72 & 73   Side (lateral) raise.*

*Figs 74 & 75    Seated press with barbell.*

## Upright Rowing (*Figs 76 and 77*)

For the muscles of the shoulders, upper back and front of upper arm.

Stand tall holding a barbell with an overgrasp so that your hands are approximately fifteen centimetres apart with the bar at arm's length in front of you. From this position, pull the bar upwards to neck height, keeping your elbows high and the bar close to your body. Hold this uppermost position for a moment, then lower the bar under control to full arm's length and repeat.

Breathe in as you raise the bar and out as you lower it.

## Heel Raise (*Figs 78 and 79*)

For the muscles of the calf.

Stand tall with a barbell resting across your shoulders/upper back, maintaining it there with a wide grip. Have the balls of your feet on two weight discs or a block of wood, yet keep your heels on the floor. Now rise up on to your toes, hold your uppermost position momentarily, then control the movement back to the starting position. Do not rest your heels down, instead, as soon as they touch the floor, repeat the sequence.

Keep your spine long throughout the exercise and breathe normally.

*Figs 76 & 77   Upright rowing.*

*Figs 78 & 79   Heel raise.*

# Back Squats
## (*Figs 80 and 81*)

For the muscles of the hips, buttocks, thighs and back.

Stand tall with your feet hip- or shoulder-width apart. Rest a barbell comfortably across your shoulders/upper back, holding it there with a wide grip. Keeping your spine long throughout and looking forward, smoothly bend your knees. Squat into a position in which your thighs are parallel to the floor, then strongly return to your starting position, making sure that you fully straighten your legs.

Breathe in as you descend and out as you rise. If you feel unstable because your heels are leaving the floor, stand with your heels on a block of wood (or two weight discs) approximately two centimetres high. Always make sure that your knees point in the same direction as your toes.

*Figs 80 & 81   Back squats.*

79

# Front Squats (*Figs 82 and 83*)

For the muscles of the hips, buttocks, thighs and back.

This is a variation of the back squat which throws more of the training emphasis on the thigh muscles and is very applicable for runners in particular.

The technique is essentially the same as for the back squat, but the bar is rested across the front of the shoulders and maintained in that position with a cross-over grip. You must keep your elbows high at all times, preferably at the same height as your shoulders. You will find that you can handle less weight than you would normally use on the back squat.

# Bench Stepping (*Fig 84*)

For the muscles of the hips, buttocks, thighs and back.

Stand tall in front of a stout, stable bench or chair with your feet approximately hip-width apart. Rest a barbell comfortably across your shoulders/upper back, holding it there with a wide grip. Place one foot fully on the bench and stand upon it, bringing the other foot up beside it, then step down.

Keep your back long throughout and breathe comfortably. After stepping up the required number of repetitions with one leg, do the same number of repetitions stepping up with the other leg.

*Figs 82 & 83    Front squats.*

Fig 84    Bench stepping.

# EXERCISES USING A MULTI-GYM AND SINGLE STATION UNITS

As indicated earlier in this book, there are many different varieties of multi-gyms and resistance-training stations. All have slightly different operating instructions and these should be referred to before you use them. The following exercises were performed using a multi-gym and simple equipment which is found in any local sports centre.

## Leg (Thigh) Extensions (*Figs 85 and 86*)

For the muscles at the front of the thigh.

Adjust your position on the machine so that when you are seated your knees are opposite the pivot point of the machine and your

Figs 85 & 86    Leg extension.

whole back is pressed firmly against the back support with your ankles behind the pads, as illustrated. Loosely grasp the side handles. Maintain this position and smoothly straighten your legs as fully as possible. Hold this position for a moment, then control the movement back to the starting position. Just before the weights touch, repeat the movement. Breathe easily throughout the exercise.

Bend your knees, still keeping your hips pressed against the bench so that your heels come towards your buttocks. Hold your furthermost position for a moment, then control the movement of your heels back to the starting position. Just before the weights touch the rest of the weight stack, repeat the movement. Keep your feet flexed throughout the exercise and breathe comfortably.

## Leg (Thigh) Curl
## (*Figs 87 and 88*)

For the muscles at the back of the thighs, and calves.

Lie face down on a leg curl machine with your heels under the roller pads and your knees opposite the machine's pivot point. Keep your hips pressed firmly against the bench and loosely grasp the side handles.

## Squat Machine – Leg Press
## (*Figs 89 and 90*)

For the muscles of the buttocks, thighs and calves.

Adjust the seat position (how you do this varies according to the type of equipment you are using) so that the angle at your knees is approximately ninety degrees. Your feet should be flat on the footplates and your

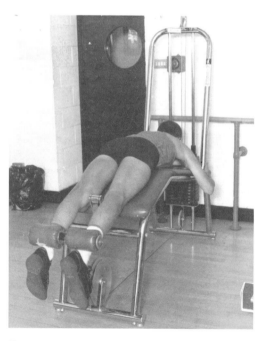
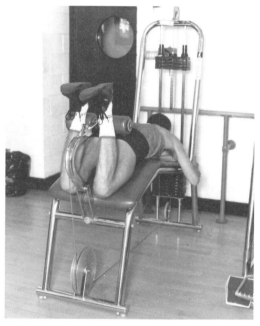

Figs 87 & 88   Leg curl.

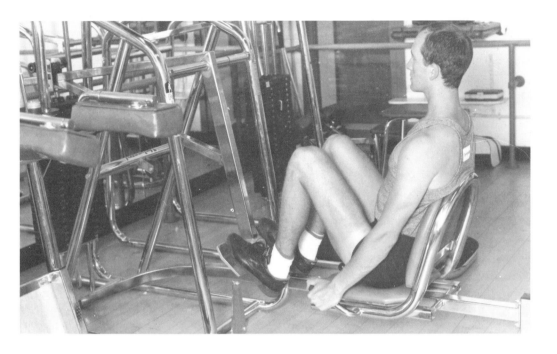

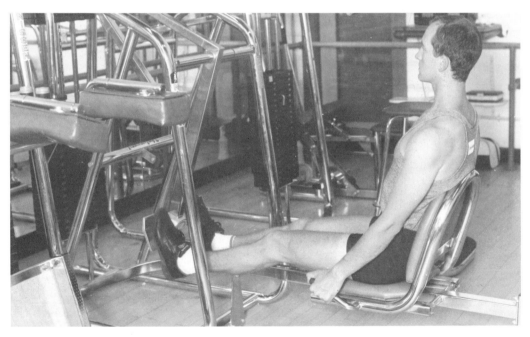

*Figs 89 & 90   Squat machine.*

lower back and shoulders must be firmly pressed into the back support. Have your hands loosely by your sides. Strongly push both feet away from you, extending your legs as fully as possible, but do not lock out your knees. Then control the movement back to your starting position. Just as the weights are about to touch the rest of the weight stack, repeat. Breathe out as you push away and breathe in on the return movement.

Some models of leg press/squat machine allow you to work each leg independently, which is useful if you think one leg is doing most of the work.

# Vertical Chest Press (*Figs 91 and 92*)

For the muscles at the front of the chest.

Adjust the seat height according to the manufacturer's instructions and check the position of the selector pin in the weight stack. Sit on the seat so that the whole of your spine is pressed firmly against the back support. Place one forearm against the appropriate arm pad and grip the handle loosely. Press this pad forward slightly, then place your other forearm against the other pad in a similar fashion. From this position, bring both

Figs 91 & 92   *Vertical chest press.*

pads together at an equal rate by pressing your forearms together. Hold the closed position momentarily before returning smoothly and under control to the starting position and repeat.

Breathe out as you bring your arms together and in on the return movement.

## Multi-Gym Squat and Heel Raise (*Figs 93 and 94*)

For the locomotor muscles of the lower body.

Many multi-gyms feature a squat/heel raise station. Other than starting from the bottom of the movement, the squat exercise is performed in the same way as the back squat using a barbell described in the previous section. The same technical rules also apply for the heel raise (described earlier).

*Figs 93 & 94    Multi-gym squat.*

## Multi-Gym Shoulder Press (*Figs 95 and 96*)

For the muscles of the upper back, shoulder and back of upper arm.

Follow instructions as for the seated shoulder press.

## Multi-Gym Bench Press (*Figs 97 and 98*)

For the muscles of the chest, front of shoulder and back of upper arm.

This exercise is essentially the same as the bench press using a barbell and the same exercise instructions apply.

## Multi-Gym Seated Row (*Figs 99 and 100*)

For the muscles of the upper back and shoulders, and front of upper arm.

Sit tall in front of the foot/heel board holding the pulley handle with an overgrasp at arm's length. Have your legs slightly bent at the knees. From this position, pull the handle towards yourself until it touches your middle, whilst keeping your spine long. Hold this position momentarily then return the handle to the starting position under control. Avoid the temptation to jerk the weight forward.

Breathe in as you pull the handle towards you and breathe out on the return.

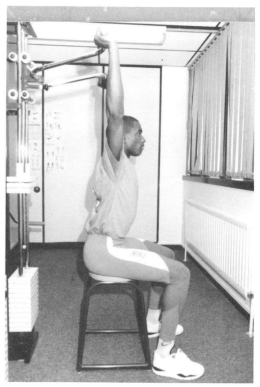

*Figs 95 & 96   Multi-Gym shoulder press.*

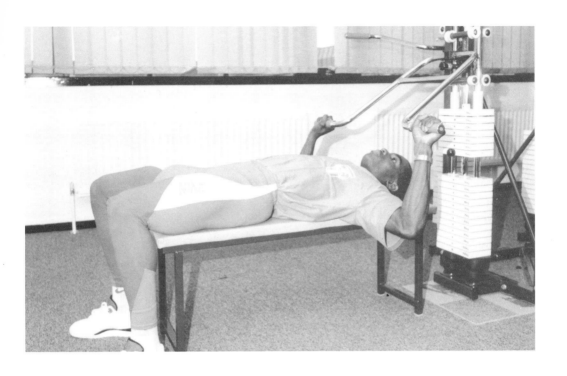

Figs 97 & 98   Multi-gym bench press.

*Figs 99 & 100   Multi-gym seated row.*

# Appendix I – Your Training Diet

To train well, you have to eat well. A good diet – for everyday life or for serious training – is one which supplies all the nutrients that the body needs in the right quantity.

To obtain the right nutrients requires a diet which is balanced and offers a wide variety of fresh and wholesome foods. The amount of food that you actually need is then determined by your size, metabolic rate and level of physical activity.

Recent reports into eating habits in the UK have revealed that few of us actually eat the right types of foods in the right quantity. Certainly we all seem to eat far too much fat and simple, refined sugars whilst not consuming enough fibre. Approximately sixty per cent of the average person's high fat intake comes from meat and dairy produce, with extra fat being added to these foodstuffs by cooking methods such as frying.

Large amounts of fat also exist in processed foods such as pies, pastries, sausages and so on and in cakes, biscuits and confectionery in general. Therefore to cut down fat intake the amount of such high fat and high calorie foods needs to be reduced, as well as changing the way that foods are cooked. Grill instead of fry and exchange high fat, often limited nutritional value foods, such as those mentioned above, with more nutritious fruit and vegetables. Substitute fatty, red meats with lean, white meats such as chicken and turkey and eat more fish. Excess fat is also added to many people's food through the far too liberal use of oils and spreads (including butter) so it also makes sense to cut down on dressings such as these, replacing them with low-fat alternatives.

To cut down on refined simple sugars stop eating so many processed foods. The more food has 'done to it', generally speaking, the less nutritious it actually is and often the more calories it contains. Eating a variety of wholefood produce, raw or simply cooked, will provide you with far more vitamins and minerals and fewer calories. The added advantage of eating more vegetables, grains and pulses is that you will consume more fibre, which aids the digestive process and you will consume more complex carbohydrates. When training, your body actually prefers a high intake of complex carbohydrates in your daily diet, because it is these which most effectively provide energy for strenuous physical activity, allowing glycogen stores to remain topped up. Furthermore, a diet high in complex carbohydrates also means that glycogen stores in the body will be replenished more rapidly, allowing subsequent training sessions that week to be performed equally effectively. Because of this, it makes sense when training hard to consume more wholegrain products such as muesli, wholemeal bread and wholemeal pasta, along with a variety of fresh vegetables, fruit and fruit juices. You should also aim to drink plenty of water, since the body can become very dehydrated when training hard (because of sweat loss).

When it comes to fitting your eating pattern around your training, remember that you should not train hard following a heavy meal, since this will lead to nausea and vomiting. Leave at least two hours between a heavy meal and hard training. However, do not go for too long without eating, since low glucose levels in the blood and depleted glycogen stores in muscles will equally impair your training. Many professional sportsmen and women prefer to eat more small meals (often six, equally spread throughout the day) rather than the traditional three large ones, with carbohydrate (and fluid) replacement occurring as soon as possible after training. This keeps up their energy levels and also ensures that adequate calories can be consumed to fuel the high volume of physical activity that they are undertaking.

Finally, many myths surround heavy training, particularly with regard to muscle size, protein consumption and vitamin and mineral supplementation. There is no need for excessive protein intake if attempting to build muscle. Increasing the size of muscles relies heavily upon the ability to train at high intensities and not upon how much protein you consume. In view of this, the foodstuff which is of most value is, once again, complex carbohydrate. A well-balanced diet, following the guide-lines given here, will also provide all of the vitamins and minerals in the right form and combination that are necessary to train effectively, making additional supplementation superfluous.

The quantity of food consumed, as already indicated, depends on a number of factors. If you keep a note of your shape and body composition as indicated on page 90, you will be able to tell whether you are consuming too many calories or not, since these measurements are much more effective when it comes to how much fat you are carrying than simply weighing yourself.

For more information on diet, exercise and fat loss, *see* the companion title, *The Complete Book of Diet and Exercise.*

# Appendix II – Your Home Gym

Many people actually prefer the idea of exercising at home, since training in this fashion means that you are not tied down to travelling to and from a sports centre or health club and you can exercise at your convenience. However, there are some drawbacks, in that certain exercises require certain items of apparatus, many of which can be costly and may indeed take up a considerable amount of space.

If you are considering setting up a home gym, then work out exactly how much available space you have, how much money you have to spend and what you intend to do. The last point should be dealt with first. If you are a regular recreational runner, it may be that the only exercises you want or need to do are simple resistance exercises involving your own body-weight or a pair of dumb-bells. The space needed for your complementary exercises can then be found easily by moving some furniture to one side. However, if you intend to get involved in body-building at home, then heavy barbells

and dumb-bells will be required, along with a bench and squat stands. Such items and the exercises which involve them take up considerable space and this needs to be taken into account. Similarly, home multi-gyms also take up quite an amount of space, as do exercise cycles, rowing machines and the like. If you are considering purchasing any of these items, firstly check that the item of equipment is well made, fits your dimensions and that you actually like it. Secondly, check that when it is in use it fits neatly into your home without having to spend hours rearranging your normal living arrangements. As a rule, the more that has to be done to set up equipment for use, the less likely it is that that equipment will be used.

For full details on the purchase and use of all kinds of home exercise equipment, plus a comprehensive guide to a vast array of exercises which can be done at home with the minimum of equipment, see the companion title *The Complete Book of Home Exercise*.

# Appendix III – Muscle Charts

To help you structure and vary your training, the exercises featured in this book are grouped here according to which main muscle/muscle groups they predominantly involve.

| Muscle/ Muscle Group | Exercise |
|---|---|
| Trapezius | Upright rowing Seated rowing Single-arm rowing |
| Deltoid | Upright rowing Shoulder press Lateral raise |
| Pectoralis major | Bench press Vertical chest press Press-ups |
| Biceps | Arm curl Alternate dumb-bell curl |
| Triceps | Bench dips |
| Latissimus dorsi | Pull-ups Seated rowing Single-arm rowing |
| Abdominal muscles | Curl-up Abdominal crunch Reverse curl 'U' sit |

| Muscle/ Muscle Group | Exercise |
|---|---|
| Spinal extensors | Hip extensions |
| Gluteal muscles, Quadriceps, Hamstrings | Hip extensions Back squats Front squats Bench stepping |
| Quadriceps | Leg extension |
| Hamstrings | Leg curl |
| Gastrocnemius | Heel raise |
| All the muscles of the lower body | Astride bench jumps Bench leaps Squat thrusts Burpees Two-footed jumps Hops Obstacle leaps Depth jumps |

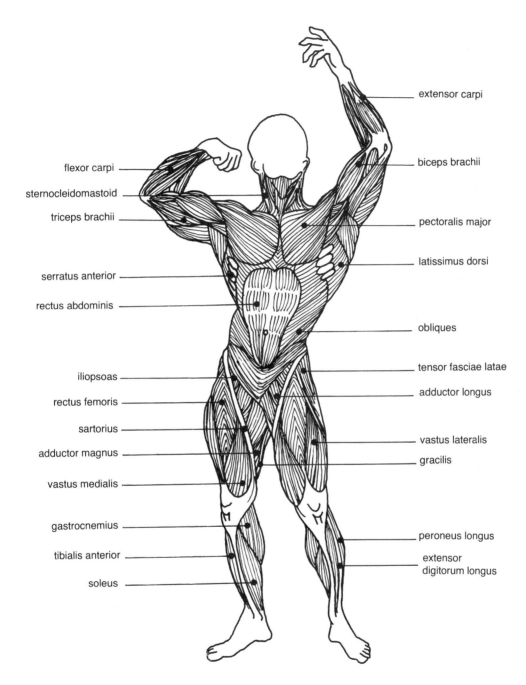

extensor carpi

biceps brachii

flexor carpi

sternocleidomastoid

triceps brachii

pectoralis major

latissimus dorsi

serratus anterior

rectus abdominis

obliques

tensor fasciae latae

iliopsoas

adductor longus

rectus femoris

sartorius

vastus lateralis

adductor magnus

gracilis

vastus medialis

gastrocnemius

peroneus longus

tibialis anterior

extensor
digitorum longus

soleus

*Figs 101 & 102   Major superficial muscle groups
of the body.*

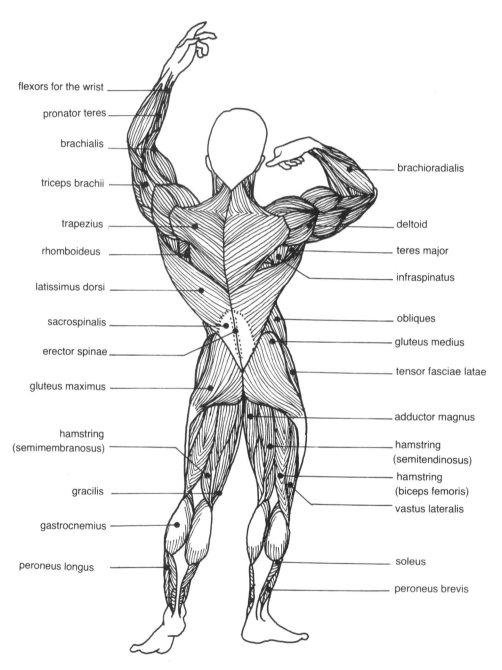

flexors for the wrist

pronator teres

brachialis

triceps brachii

trapezius

rhomboideus

latissimus dorsi

sacrospinalis

erector spinae

gluteus maximus

hamstring
(semimembranosus)

gracilis

gastrocnemius

peroneus longus

brachioradialis

deltoid

teres major

infraspinatus

obliques

gluteus medius

tensor fasciae latae

adductor magnus

hamstring
(semitendinosus)

hamstring
(biceps femoris)

vastus lateralis

soleus

peroneus brevis

Fig 102